Ho.

Guide to rishing Northern Arkansas,
Southern Missouri and Western Tennessee

Copyright© 1993
All Rights Reserved
Mid-South Fly Fishers
Memphis, Tennessee
ISBN 1-882626-15-X

Printed in the United States of America
This first edition published by arrangement with
Impressions Ink, Inc.
5147 Patrick Henry Dr.
Memphis, TN 38134
(901) 388-5382

FEDERATION OF
FLY FISHERS

Home Waters is a compilation of fishing experience collected over a period of years from many individuals fishing the regions. Great effort has been taken to credit all sources used in this guide. Any omission should be directed to Mid-South Fly Fishers c/o Impressions Ink, Inc.

Foreword

by Dave Whitlock

The Ozarks, my home waters, are one of the most unique, lovely and interesting areas to flyfish as any I've discovered in the world. I've spent most of my life unraveling it's secrets, and am still learning about this area each time I drive, hike, canoe, wade or swim the fantastic variety of outdoor areas. I feel comfortable, safe, relaxed and content here...more than any other place I've spent time, and that's for good reason. I know my way with the people, roads, weather and waters. For the visitor, prospective visitor or local just beginning to flyfish here, it can be just the opposite, uncomfortable, hazardous and frustrating, if you get on the wrong path. That is exactly why *Home Waters* has been written. To insure that those inexperienced to this area can have a clear, concise and truthful guide to these flyfishing waters. A guide that gives you the perspective and the dimensions and potentials available in the Ozark country.

Home waters is a guide book that contains the information that would take you or I ten to twenty years of our lives and thousands of dollars to compile by personal experience. It is easy to read, study and refer to. It is an orientation course that will prepare you to get the most out of your interests here and it would make the ideal gift to any friend that you want to share the Ozarks with. The Mid-South Fly Fishers, with this book, are doing the fly fishers a very special service and most personal favor with this highly detailed, informative system.

Because flyfishing in the mid-south is still a very minority angling method, many services people, guides, tackle shops and resorts here, are inexperienced in the sport and can often mislead or discourage you as you seek help from them. So, my advice is to read *Home Waters* because it will give you the base of flyfishing information that will prevent this pitfall...so consider it Ozark fly fishing insurance.

Arkansas' environmental and game laws, and small enforcement staff makes the state among the most lax in America, and very vulnerable to exploitation, pollution and poaching. I honestly believe that this area does not need one more tourist, angler or new resident using our fragile resources unless they are prepared to give the special care the area needs and deserves. So please, if you visit or move here, as they say, help us by being part of the solution rather than the problem here. Obey our laws and respect our land and waters and all that evolve around their health and quality. Please support our efforts to conserve and improve the mid-south's treasure...our Home Waters. Good Ozark flyfishing.

Preface

In 1990 the Mid-South Fly Fishers produced a book called Home Waters of the Mid-South Fly Fishers. The book was intended to assist new and experienced anglers in the club "find and successfully fish the major trout and warm waters in the Mid-South area". It featured articles, maps and fly recipes and was given free to all club members.

Our club has now grown to over 250 members and there is both more knowledge and more thirst for information about our fisheries. As we discussed reprinting our simple reference we explored whether others would benefit from the book. Many non-club members have inquired about the book. Several fly fishing guides and shop owners have noted that there is no reference book for the grouping of fisheries in this book.

Also figuring in our decision was the increasing interest of club members to participate in educational and conservation programs. It is clear that to protect our fisheries we need more education and we need to educate others. Additionally we need to be involved in more conservation efforts to preserve the fragile fisheries for the future.

In deciding to offer this book to those of you outside our club we want you to know that the **proceeds will finance educational and conservation programs.** This will benefit you as well as the fish we all enjoy catching and releasing.

Acknowledgments

The vision and development of this book came from the grassroots of our Mid-South Fly Fishers club. What started as a perk for our membership has grown into a major publishing effort which we hope anglers from all over the country enjoy.

In addition to the authors listed with their articles, many club members contributed to its success. The professional "look" is due in large part to Art Terry, who handled layout and design and Phyllis Bailey our "artist-in-residence" who drew all the flies. Alan Ford took the maps developed by Paul Pettit and updated them for our new format. Anita Nobles shared her knowledge of publishing and promotion and guided us through the steps. The Home Waters committee put in untold hours researching, writing and proofing: Phyllis Bailey, Judy Boston, Larry Conatser, Peter Fox, Travis Handwerker, Rod Hardinger, Bill Lax, Ben Leggett, Tracie Maler, Roger Maler, Anita Nobles, George Owen, John Simank and Art Terry.

A special thanks to our "fishing experts" President Jim Bailey, Past Presidents Mike Pollard, John Berry, and Jim Cowan, and club member Dan Berry for reviewing the book for its fishing accuracy. Also, thanks to C.B. Nance, George Harmeling, Paul Pettit and our fishing experts for providing us with a history of our club.

The cover art was donated by club member and president Monte Stark of The Sporting Life. This beautiful water color of three trout by Mike Stidham truly captures the beauty of our sport.

Sharing support and encouragement were Missouri angler, hydrologist, and writer Chuck Tryon and Arkansas professional fly fisher, author, and educator, Dave Whitlock.

Finally we want to thank the members and Board of Directors of the Mid-South Fly Fishers for their support of this project and their readiness to allow us to bounce ideas off of them.

We hope you enjoy this book as much as we did putting it together. We believe it will bring you many hours of fishing and reading enjoyment.

Jennifer Jenkins
Vice President of the Mid-South Fly Fishers, and
Chairperson of the *Home Waters Committee*

Contents

Cold Water

History of the
Mid-South Fly Fishers

In July 1977, the Mid-South Fly Fishers was incorporated as a non-profit organization under the laws of the State of Arkansas. Twenty adults and one youth member met over a fish fry in West Memphis, Arkansas. Over the years the changing meeting place reflected the changing membership. Initially meeting in West Memphis, the group added many new members from Memphis. The meeting sites migrated to Midtown Memphis, Tennessee and later to Germantown, on the far east side of Memphis. Membership is now in excess of 265 and includes members from Tennessee, Arkansas, and Mississippi.

All original members of the club were members of the Federation of Fly Fishers. Today the club is an active member club of the Federation and is one of the larger clubs in the Southern Council. Several club members have received awards from the Federation for their work: The "Man of the Year" award was given to George Harmeling (twice) and Paul Pettit. Peggy Pettit received the "Woman of the Year" award twice.

Keeping members informed has always been important and the first newsletter was published in September of 1977. Club members regularly contribute articles to our "Tight Lines & Tall Tales" which are both informative and humorous.

As the membership grew, many people joined who were not expert fly fishers or who just wanted to learn fly fishing and tying. As early as 1977 the club began sponsoring educational sessions. Paul Pettit offered the first fly tying class in West Memphis. Today the club offers two fly fishing classes a year (attended by 30-45 individuals), two fly tying classes, a rod building class, and an annual seminar with a nationally known speaker. Some of our esteemed speakers have been Dave Whitlock, Gary Borger, Doug Swisher, Chico Fernandez, Jack Dennis, Trey Combs, Jimmy Nix, and Lefty Kreh.

In addition, each monthly club meeting has a speaker or program designed to inform the members. Increasingly these programs are focusing on habitat preservation and conservation efforts.

In 1979 the club, in cooperation with the Arkansas Fly Fishers of Little Rock, introduced Brown trout from Montana to the Little Red River. With the Heber Springs airport fogged in, they made a late night dash to the Little Rock airport to retrieve the trout fry and take them immediately to the Little Red for planting. The stocking was repeated in 1981. The fact that the world record Brown trout (40 lbs. 4 oz) was caught in 1992 on the Little Red River is testimony to the program's success.

In 1988, the Mid-South Fly Fishers in conjunction with the Arkansas Fly Fishers of Little Rock raised $2000 each to purchase property on the Little Red River at Cow Shoals. This effort, as a memorial to club member Bill Leaptrott (photographer with the former Memphis Press Scimitar and the Commercial Appeal), has established a permanent public access through the Arkansas Game & Fish Commission for future generations.

In 1993 the club worked with the Little Rock club again to clip fins on 20,000 Rainbows at the National Trout Fishery in Norfork, Arkansas. These efforts will permit better long-term monitoring of trout habits, growth, and migration. The club also worked with the Arkansas Fish & Game Commission to produce "Trout Tips: A Guide for Handling & Releasing Trout". This card is given to everyone buying an Arkansas trout stamp. We hope that it will inform more people about catch and release and increase the number of trout returned to our streams in healthy condition. An excerpt can be found in the next article in our book called "Catch and Release".

The purpose of the Mid-South Fly Fishers, as stated in its Articles of Incorporation is:

"To improve and increase the sport of fly fishing in the Mid-South; to encourage and advocate the conservation in the waters of the Mid-South; to encourage and assist others to become fly fishers and true sportspersons; to promote the pleasure and fellowship of its members and to engage in such activities as may be necessary and expedient for the achievement of the above stated purposes."

Catch and Release

During the past decade sales in fishing licenses and trout stamps have dramatically increased. As fishing pressure increases in our "home waters", the hatchery-based system cannot maintain the demand for fish. Funding once available for stocking programs is competing for the ever shrinking state and federal dollar. Historically there has been more emphasis on harvest management programs rather than protection of the resources such as fisheries habitat preservation and restoration.

As the *Home Waters* publication guides you along the Arkansas, Tennessee, and Missouri waters, help us preserve the quality of the Mid-South fishery by practicing catch and release. Trout grow very rapidly in our home waters, but they must be returned to the water to do so. Arkansas has produced two world record Brown trout, one each from the Norfork and Little Red Rivers during recent years. Catch and release insures that you have exactly what you are looking for while fishing — large populations of large fish.

The Mid-South Fly Fishers and the Arkansas Fish & Game Commission developed the following guide for handling and releasing trout:

1. Use barbless hooks or use pliers to flatten barbs on regular hooks.

2. Land the fish as quickly as possible.

3. When unhooking the fish, keep it in the water as long as possible.

4. Don't squeeze the fish.

5. Don't stick your fingers in the fish's gills.

6. Wet your hands if you need to hold the fish.

7. If you hold the fish, hold it in front of its tail or cradle it upside down in your palm.

8. If the fish has swallowed the hook, cut the line as close to the hook as possible.
9. Gently hold the fish in the water allowing it to reacclimate before releasing it.
10. Report all violations you see: in Arkansas (800) 482-9262, in Tennessee (800) 255-TWRA, and in Missouri (800) 392-1111.

We encourage you to practice catch and release, for the preservation of our resources and for everyone's enjoyment .

Bill Theodorou
Editor, *Tight Lines & Tall Tales*
Mid-South Fly Fishers Newsletter

COLD WATER

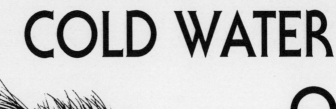

COLD WATER

COLD WATER

COLD WATER

COLD WATER

Safety

On the White, Norfork and Little Red Rivers water flow is dramatically affected by the generation of electricity at the dams. Fishers should be cautioned that while the Corps of Engineers sounds a horn at the dam prior to turning on the generators, this cannot be heard further downstream. As with any tail water fishery, this necessitates extreme caution on the part of fishers. The water can (and does) rise one or more feet in 10-15 minutes. Carry a whistle to alert other fishers and to call for assistance if you need it. When fishing the tail water fisheries, always plan your quickest and safest way to leave the river - if necessary go to the far bank and flag down another fisher to pick you up in a boat or to go get help.

While fishing pick out a rock which you can monitor every few minutes. If the sound of the water in riffles or runs changes and/or you note that the water is rising on your rock, head for shore. Felt bottom wading boots are highly recommended. Always carry and use a wading staff. When using a staff you have three points of contact with the bottom. Never move but one point at a time. The bottom is slick and the staff helps you find holes before you step in. This is particularly important when the water is rising. You may not be able to cross back over water you just did if the water comes up since holes you just waded may now be too deep.

The water temperature is usually in the 50's. If you fall in, you are in danger of hypothermia. Once out of the water, get dry as soon as possible. Carry extra dry clothes in your car. It is a good idea to carry matches in a waterproof container to use to build a fire if you get stranded on the far shore and no one is available to help you.

In addition to water safety, don't forget to take your sunglasses, sun screen, and a hat. These items will add to your enjoyment of the sport and provide additional protection against the elements.

The White, Norfork, and Little Red Rivers are fun to fish, however, it is important to respect the power of the water and remember that the river always seems to come up after you have waded for some time and are tired. This makes it more important for you to be cautious. Follow these simple guidelines and have a wonderful time.

Note: For information on how to fish during high water, refer to Dale Fulton's article in this book.

Flyfishing High Water - White and Norfork Rivers

By Dale Fulton

As the demand for hydropower has increased over the last few years, it has become necessary for fly fishers to develop techniques for fishing the higher water levels. The techniques, though simple, are only effective if used in conjunction with knowledge of the rivers, and gaining this knowledge takes time. Here are a few tips and suggestions to help get you started in this fascinating aspect of tailwater fly fishing:

BOATS - A boat is the single most important piece of equipment for high water flyfishing. There is some wading available in any of the water levels, but to be really effective you must fish from a boat. Any safe boat will be of some help, even including canoes and small jon boats, but the most useful boats are the standard 20' fiberglass jon boats commonly seen on the White and Norfork Rivers. A 9.8 horsepower outboard works perfectly on these boats. Make sure the boat is equipped with fuel, paddles, and all required safety gear, but try and keep the decks and floor as uncluttered as possible to avoid tangling your line.

TACKLE and RIGGING - Fly rods for high water fishing should be at least 8'-6"to 9' long and a 6 to 8 weight. Six weight rods are ideal for drift fishing but 7 and 8 weight rods are better for throwing big streamers. You should have a floating line for your lighter rod and both floating and sink tip or full sinking lines for the heavier rods. On your floating line leaders should be 9' to 12'(occasionally even longer), with tippets from 3X to 5X. Use a strike indicator set deeper than the water you are fishing and split shot from size B to 3/0, depending on the current speed.

On the sinking outfit I use a level section of 2X or 3X tippet about

5' long. Attach a permanent loop to the sinking end of your fly line and tie the tippet directly to it.

FLIES - For drift fishing (dead drift with a strike indicator) a good rule of thumb is *the higher the water, the brighter the fly.* Most of your standard low water patterns will work well in the lower flows (up to 40% of the dam's capacity). My favorites are Sowbugs, Hare's ears, Prince nymphs, and Bighorn shrimp, in sizes 10 to 14. As the flows increase to 100% (yes, that does mean eight generators) the brighter flies, like Glo bugs and San Juan worms, will become more effective. The main high water diet of large Brown trout is either sculpin or shad that have washed through the dam from the lake above, so focus your streamer patterns on these in size 2 to 6. The fish also feed heavily on crayfish, but so far I've had little luck with them.

THE RIVERS - In our tailwater rivers the water is either rising, falling (called a tailwater, hence the name), or stable. As a very general rule, fish feed heaviest in rising water, usually feed intermittently in stable water, and poorly in falling water. Wading fishers are most often fishing falling water and leave when the water begins to rise. In any given spot, the water will often take from 1 to 4 hours to rise completely and become stable. If the rising water is fishing well, move downstream to stay with it. If for some reason the rise isn't fishing well, move far upstream to get into stable high water.
As you fish through the day in stable high water you often will notice the fish going through periods of feeding. If you pay attention you will see that these periods correspond with small changes in the level of the already high water. Learn to recognize and take advantage of these small changes by moving with them up and down the river.

Where to Fish—

DRIFT FISHING - Tailwater trout are lazy and will always move away from the full force of the current. Rainbows will feed over a gravel bottom in current that has been slightly slowed by islands, underwater gravel bars, levees and breakwaters, big rocks, the tails of the pools (pools in low water), and the inside bends of the river. The key here is to learn to recognize these slightly slower areas. If you can see current breaks so much the better, but many of them are hidden in high water. Use your knowledge of the river bottom in low water but don't be concerned that you are fishing areas that you normally walk on: people view the wild fluctuation of the tailwaters as unnatural, but the trout don't. To them, its as natural as day and night.

STREAMER FISHING - With the exception of their spawning period, when they are found near gravel bars, Brown trout like cover. Look for medium depth rock bottom areas with rocks and logs for cover. Throw streamers with sinking or sink tip lines close, and I do mean close, to the cover and strip your fly back. Generally a fast retrieve works best but try different speeds. Often when the trout are feeding on shad an extremely slow retrieve works well. You'll know when you get a strike.

FISHING FROM A BOAT - Its sometimes difficult for fly fishers to accept the fact that when fishing from a boat, boat handling skill is as important as fishing skill. If you're new to boats allow yourself time to learn and develop your boat handling skill. For the best success fishing, one person must be handling the boat at all times. Take turns, and when its your turn to drive the boat, put your rod away. The easiest way to handle the boat for both drift fishing and streamer fishing is with the bow pointed upstream and the motor idling. Use the motor to position the boat for casting. The motor doesn't seem to scare the fish and its handy to have it running if you get in a tight spot. As you get more experienced try using a paddle (less noise and exhaust fumes), but don't underestimate the skill and strength needed to move a twenty foot boat. For drift fishing try to match the boat speed to the speed of the current to get the longest possible drift. Often you will have to shift the motor in and out of gear to accomplish this.

SAFETY and COURTESY - The two things that contribute most to boating safety (other than the obvious required safety gear) are caution and experience. The rule here is gain your experience cautiously. Take your time, don't get flustered, and enjoy the learning process. You are required by regulation to have a wearable life jacket within easy reach of each person in the boat. Since it has to be there anyway, put it on! It won't do you any good lying in the bottom of the boat, and your line will just get tangled in it anyway. Start your high water flyfishing with safety as your main concern and as you learn it will become second nature. If you're unsure of trying it by yourself, by all means hire a guide for a day to show you the ropes. For perspective, one last point: There are few things more dangerous than wading in a river that can rise eight feet without warning.

We've all heard stories of rude boaters in low water. Don't become one. This is your chance to teach river courtesy by example. Enough said.

Common Mistakes

Anchoring - Trying to anchor a boat in the swift waters of our rivers will get you dead. Don't even think about it.

Everyone fishing, no one operating the boat - This is a good way to not catch any fish and get in trouble to boot. For effective fishing and safety, have one person operating the boat at all times.

Casting too much - Fly fishers love to cast, but you need your fly in the water to allow plenty of time to sink.

Sinking strike indicator - Use enough strike indicator to float dry through your longest possible drift. Its confusing and shortens your drift to have a sinking indicator.

Indicator set too deep - Even though the rivers are fast and deep, many of the areas that you want to fish are only 2' to 5' deep. Use a very deep indicator setting only in deep water.

Buying a boat - Rent boats until your skill at boat handling surpasses the quality of the boats available to rent. Tailwater rivers are hard on expensive boats and motors, even with skillful boat handling.

There is much more to be learned about fly fishing high water. Hopefully this information, which was definitely not come by easily, can get you started and you can help refine the techniques. I hope to see you out there. I'll be the one in the old green boat, catching fish. Good luck!

Night Fishing

by Mike Pollard

With the exception of fishing for trophy browns over their spawning beds, most Mid-South fly fishers rarely get the chance to cast to really big trout — the size of fish that can make braggarts out of the most meek among us. This is usually the case not because of a lack of fishing acumen, but because of the increased pressures that all of our rivers are experiencing, and because of the preferred nocturnal life-style of these fish.

So, the next time you're out on the river at dusk, don't let darkness intimidate you and run you off the river. Instead, follow the prescribed safety guidelines and fishing strategies outlined here and get ready to experience some mighty fine fishing.

To begin, night fishing is not for the faint of heart, nor can it be successful if one does not possess patience or keen observation skills. In addition, anyone attempting to fish by the night light shimmering off the river should already have mastered the basics of the cast, knot tying, fly presentation, and wading techniques. The dark will truly magnify any faults you have.

In selecting water to fish, safety must be your first rule. Therefore, choose pools or slow moving riffles that you know well. If a section of water looks good, get to know it during the daylight so you can remember the sweet spots that will hold fish. Note the boulders and weed beds, and develop a perspective of the width and length of its fishing area. If you're going to fish one of the tailwaters, call the dam before you pull up to your parking spot so you don't have to immediately worry about rising water.

In selecting specific water, the tailouts of long, slow pools with a deep spot in the middle of the pool are ideal. These will be more likely to hold larger fish which will move back to the tailout to feed. This is where they will best be able to corner bait fish and sip spinners in the smooth converging currents of the glide. If you can find this type of location that also has some existing light source such as bridges, boat docks, dam sites, or street lights, so much the better.

The tailout at the Little Red's swinging bridge section is one such place. Another is the section below McClellan's trout dock on the Norfork. Also, there are several tailouts along the campgrounds at JFK park, and at the dam site on the Little Red.

The classic approach to fishing these spots is to locate yourself slightly upstream and to the side of the tailout. Slow your casting stroke down a little to open up your casting loop, and this will help eliminate many of the problems you may experience with tangled leaders and flies. Cast slightly upstream and allow your fly to drift naturally, trying to keep as much slack out of the line as possible. Try to keep your rod tip pointed in the direction of your fly, although sometimes this may be guesswork. The attempt is to show the trout a broad side profile of your fly. Once it has swung through the converging currents below you, slowly strip the fly back in one-inch to two inch nice strips. The key is to get a natural drift, and to work your fly slowly through the water.

Even during the blackest of new moon nights, there is some light on the water, although it may be elusive and feeble. To take advantage of it, periodically get down close to river level and locate the reflections, or wade to places from which you can best use the angle of the light. Look both up and down the river to determine your best possible spot. In many situations, you may be able to detect the movement or wakes of feeding fish. If you see or hear feeding fish, try to make your presentation 8 to 10 feet up river of the fish and drift the fly through the strike zone. Work your area slowly. If you don't spook the fish, you'll get many chances to catch your trophy. Keep in mind that it may be beneficial to rest the pool every five to ten minutes.

While night fishing, keep the length of your cast between 20 to 30 feet and vary its length as little as possible. This way, you'll be able to determine the location of your fly even if you can't see it at the end of your cast through repetition of the same casting distance.

If you get to an opportunity to stalk feeding fish, don't make the mistake of thinking that the night will cover up sloppy wading. The only thing that will put down a trophy size trout faster than your wakes or splashy steps is any flash of light you make with a lighter or pocket maglight. Your flashlight should only be used to find your way down to the river, or your way back to your car. Don't use it to locate fish. If you have to use a light while on the water, turn to face the bank while trying to conceal as much of the light as possible. Also, by putting a red lens on your light source you'll reduce the amount of night blindness you'll experience.

Another effective strategy to use in locating and hooking a lot of feeding trout — although usually not the trophies — is to fish slow, shallow river channels below a riffle. Wade within 25 feet of the channel, and cast your fly across the channel and slightly upstream. As the fly lands, toss a small downstream mend into the line. This puts a downstream bow in the line, which pulls the fly a little faster than the current. When the fish takes the fly, usually all you will feel is a slight hesitation in the drift. At this moment, set the hook and get ready to get wet. Most fish caught at night will tend to spend most of their time fighting near the surface, and the experience of a 12-inch rainbow at night will rival the experience of any 16-inch fish caught in daylight. The narrow channels at the state park section and the lower section of Wild Cat Shoals on the White River are two good locations. Another choice spot is Little Red's Cow Shoals area directly down from the access trail.

In terms of equipment, use a rod you are comfortable with and know well. An 8-foot, 6/7 weight equipped with a WF floating line and 4X 7-foot leader is standard. If you use the larger flies listed at the end

of this article, you'll want to terminate with a 3X tippet. Carry a net and several rigged tippets with flies to make your fly changes easier. And, above all, leave your fly vest in the car. Keep your fishing as simple as possible. Spend your time concentrating on hearing feeding fish, and on catching the shimmering wakes of their movement. Walk the banks and don't be afraid to try different locations if one doesn't pan out. Fish have feeding periods during the night just as they have during the day.

The closer to the new moon phase you are, the better fishing you will experience. A good alternative can be cloudy nights during the full moon phase. But if it's a partly cloudy night, you'll usually experience slow periods when the moon comes out.

Night fishing can be a special time on your favorite river. You can usually have the river to yourself, or share it with a friend. And, if you listen closely, you'll probably hear a fly line swishing through the air, or a reel screaming out in the quiet darkness down the river from you. When you do, you'll know where I am.

Wet flies (non-weighted)

   * Professor, Size 8
   * Lead Wing Coachman, Size 8 Dry Flies
   * Salmon Bomber, Size 6
   * Muddler (coated with floatant), Size 4
   * Deer Hair Mouse, Size 2-6
   * Deer Hair Frog, Size 6 Nymphs (non-weighted)
   * Damsel nymph (olive), Size 10 Streamers (weighted)
   * Black Wooly Bugger, Size 2-8
   * Olive Brown Sculpin, Size 2

Dear Trout Enthusiast:

Greetings from the Natural State! I hope each of you will visit our state and sample Arkansas' trout fisheries. We currently have 5 year round large streams, 4 large reservoirs, and several smaller streams or seasonal fisheries to chose from.

Our larger streams such as Bull Shoals, Norfork, Greer's Ferry (Little Red River) and Beaver Tailwaters as well as the Spring River comprise 137 miles of the Southeastern United States' finest trout fishing. These rivers have produced 9 world class line records for brown trout including the all tackle world record of 40 pounds 4 ounces from the Little Red River.

Exciting developments are also underway in an attempt to further diversify trout fishing opportunities in Arkansas. I have set a goal of locating at least one catch and release or highly restricted harvest area on each of the 5 large streams by 1995. These areas will be selected to produce lunker sized rainbow and cutthroat trout of 5 pounds or more.

Effective January 1, 1993 we also put cutthroat trout under special regulations identical to that of brown trout (2 fish per day, 16 inch length). Coupled with the re-introduction of a superior strain of cutthroat we anticipate that we can offer world class cutthroat in 3-4 years. Plans have been made to also introduce brook trout to Norfork and Spring River in limited numbers. Experimental stocking indicates that these fish attain 16-19 inches and 2-3 pounds within 3 years.

We are also planning to develop several small stream trout fisheries that may be under restrictive regulations. If that's not enough for you why not try fishing for trout in Bull Shoals, Hamilton, Catherine, or Ouachita Lakes? Although little known, Bull Shoals Lake in particular offers charter fishing for rainbow running 1-5 pounds.

One further note: recent developments should greatly reduce or eliminate some historic limiting factors (oxygen in particular) of our tailwater fisheries which should further enhance the super productivity of these waters.

Hope to see you soon!

Sincerely,

John Stark
Arkansas' Trout Biologist

LITTLE RED RIVER

Little Red River

by Duane Hada

The Little Red River is located two and one-half hours northwest of Memphis, Tennessee, in northcentral Arkansas, one hour from Little Rock, and forty miles from Batesville. It begins as a tailwater below Greer's Ferry Dam at Heber Springs, and flows in an easterly direction beyond Heber Springs, through the Libby and Pangburn areas in White county. This blue ribbon stream's trout waters end a few miles beyond the Ramsey Access.

Little Red River

The following is a compilation of two articles submitted to Home Waters by Duane Hada, one of the premier guides on the Little Red River who has much valuable experience.

The Little Red River is a real gem among trout rivers. Starting at the base of Greer's Ferry Dam, trout waters extend some thirty plus miles below offering the fly angler a wide variety of water types and fishing challenges. Water released from the depths of Greer's Ferry lake enter the Little Red in a range of the low to mid 50 degree mark. This controlled environment results in optimum level growth rates for trout on a year round basis. These excellent growing conditions have produced Rainbows from upwards of 15 lbs. to the existing World Record Brown trout of 40 lbs./4oz. The Little Red truly has the potential to produce quantities of maximum size trout on par with the best trout waters of the world. Keep in mind that a lot of land on the river is posted private and should be treated as such. Use the public access areas or travel the river by boat to reach other parts of the river. Public access areas include: JFK Park at the dam, Barnett (Swinging Bridge), Cow Shoals, Libby Shoals, Lobo Landing, Dripping Springs, Pangburn Bridge, and Ramsey Access.

Rainbow trout were first introduced into the Little Red River after the completion of Greer's Ferry Dam, which forever changed the character of the natural river. These hatchery trout found conditions to their liking and flourished on an abundance of food and relatively low fishing pressure. Many remember the large catches of lunker size, full-bodied Rainbows of the mid-60's through the early 80's. Many 10 pound and over Rainbows were taken from the river during this period. Lunker boards at the docks gave recognition for trophy Rainbows over four pounds which were taken from the river. A "Catch & Release" patch was started a short time later.

Brown trout have become the real success story of the Little Red River. This is the brain-child of dedicated, future-minded Fly fishers from the Memphis and Little Rock areas. From egg planting and fry stocking in the late-70's wild Brown trout have taken hold in the river. They have recently made their mark on history with a world record fish. Wild specimens of Salmo Trutta (Brown Trout) from the Little Red River have some of the most striking coloration and markings found within the species. Through increased natural reproduction, we have seen the spread of the Brown trout population range over most of the trout water on the Little Red. Each year more and larger Browns are taken further down river.

The wild stream bred Browns of the Little Red give a fly angler a chance to encounter a fish of true trophy standards. These fish are scattered throughout the upper half of the river over most of the year.

Cutthroat trout, a native fish to the western mountainous waters have found their way to the Little Red through stockings of fingerlings by the Arkansas Fish and Game Commission. The first plantings were in the early 1990s. Very susceptible to angling pressure, many were quickly harvested. Occasionally an acclimated sizable Cutthroat is caught. They are beautiful fish, fine spotted with gold olive sides, orange fins, a rosy cheek and the telltale bright orange slashes under the gill plates. As of this writing, 16-20 inchers have been caught. A real trophy should show up in the near future if the population holds.

Occasionally other fish are taken in the Little Red, so don't be too surprised by what you catch. Good populations of Chain Pickerel exist in the river and Spotted Bass are fairly common. Crappie and various Sunfish exist and on occasion Walleye show up. Lake Trout and Hybrid Stripers have found their way into the river and have provided a great surprise for anglers. The Rainbow, Brown and Cutthroat Trout are the most commonly sought after species.

The Little Red has all of the water types you can imagine. Many areas are shallow and weedy, with clear, slow moving, currents, not unlike Big Spring Creek. Bolder strewn, swift shoals can also be found in a few areas. More common are the long, deep holes with heavy coontail moss beds and log jams along the banks. These make excellent cover areas to hide and grow trout to trophy potential. The stream bed is composed of sandy soil with a good amount of dark boulders and chunk rock scattered about, covered with a permanent coating of moss. Large gravel beds and washouts can be found on many of the shoal areas. The further one travels downstream the more the character of the river changes. It is most notable below Pangburn where Big Spring Creek feeds into the river. At this point the river flows out of the Ozark Foothills and enters the flood plains of the White River. Water clarity lessens and temperature increases slightly as does the variety of fish species. A unique feature to most trout anglers is the large stands of Cypress trees growing along the banks in the lower stretch of the trout water, a sure reminder that this is a southern trout stream.

The Little Red River is a year round fishery. Knowing the changes in the seasons and water patterns along with food types and abundances can make for more successful fishing.

The Little Red is an excellent river for those who enjoy hunting trout or stalking and sight casting to an individual fish. Most of my large trout have been taken in this manner. The ability to spot fish underwater is essential to being successful with this technique. At times large trout will move out of the deep pockets and holes on the river to cruise the banks and moss beds for Sow Bugs. These fish can be extremely spooky in low, clear water. Careful, accurate casts, long tippets without indicators are the best ways to get hits. You must watch the fish carefully for the subtle take.

Many other flies and techniques will work on this river much the same as on any other stream. Wooly Buggers stripped along the bottom or just under the surface can bring strong hits at times. We have found a sparsely dressed soft hackle fished on the swing to be deadly during a Caddis hatch when they're not taking on the surface.

Fly fishing at night can be quite a successful experience on the Little Red at times. Make sure your casting is practiced to the point where you can rely on the feel of the rod for your timing. It is wise to know the water conditions at the dam and stay alert to changes. To take fish at night we have found flies that give off a wake or make a sound catch most fish. Straight 9' 3X leader with large black Wooly Buggers with rubber legs added out the sides have been the most successful for us. We have also taken some nice Browns fishing surface deer hair bugs on occasion. While some spectacular catches have been made, I haven't found it to be as consistent as daytime fishing. If it sounds like something for you, give it a try, be alert, be careful. Try to keep your light off the water as much as possible. A couple of years ago we were filming a night fly fishing episode on the Little Red. The camera crew had to use a strong light to film and we didn't catch any fish. After a couple of hours, we decided to give it up and went to another pool where we just fished (without filming). We began catching fish immediately. The camera crew wanted to get one of my guides with a large Brown on film. That was the last fish. The light put them down.

The Sow Bug (Cress Bug) is the main item on the menu for trout in the Little Red. Large quantities are found in the stomach samples from fingerlings to trophy fish. Look in a mossy, rocky area along the entire length of the river and you will find this flattened, pill-shaped morsel that is the Red River trout staple. Some of the largest concentrations can be seen in the JFK Park stretch where at times the stream bottom is literally crawling with tiny gray and tan shapes. Deep bodied trout are usually not far behind.

Sow Bugs are found in the stream and are fed on by trout all year long. With the abundance of Sow Bugs, one wonders why a fly fisher needs to be concerned with imitating anything else. Believe me, a Sow Bug imitation should be in your arsenal of flies and used frequently, but other food forms, both aquatic and terrestrial exist and should not be ignored. At times, usually in the spring months, massive hatches that rival anything seen in the West occur on the Little Red. Most of these are in the middle to lower stretches of the river where there are slightly warmer temperatures and a silt covered bottom. Large quantities of Caddis are frequently encountered along with March Browns, Cahills/Sulfurs, and Blue Winged Olives.

Midge hatches occur heavily from the base of the dam throughout the river, but the heaviest midging seems to occur in the JFK Park area, especially in the late fall through winter. When we conduct clinics on the river one thing we always have the students do is to screen the water. They are always amazed at the amount and variety of food we find in the Little Red. Samples reveal a variety of aquatic worms and leeches, snails, damsel nymphs, crawfish, scuds, grass shrimp, bait fish fry, assorted mayfly nymphs, and caddis cases. Even large Golden Stonefly nymphs are often gathered around the mouth of Big Creek.

The Little Red also experiences some wonderful terrestrial fishing, usually in summer and the early fall months. Small bright green leaf hoppers are found all along the grassy banks of the river and are constantly finding their way into the water. Ants are another food that I have seen the trout feed on at this time of year. I recall a day on the river when the Tent Caterpillars were falling and we watched the Browns surface feed on them from the deck of a friend's home. Sight casting with a terrestrial can be some of the most exciting fishing you can experience on the river.

Most fly fishers will find that the Little Red is an excellent nymphing river. A Sow Bug rigged on a light tippet below an indicator and allowed to dead drift drag free, barely above the bottom will usually catch fish of all sizes consistently. Match the natural Sow Bug in both size and color, adjust tippet length, and use microshot to stay in the strike zone. There are a handful of fly fishers who have mastered this technique on the Little Red and believe me you won't want to fish their second hand water. It's an imitation of the natural common food fished in a natural manner. What could be more effective? (*Note most fly fishers limit themselves to shallow water shoal areas—give the deep slow moving weed bed areas a try with this technique.)

Small midge pupa fished on a greased leader and fine tippet can save the day on super finicky surface feeders which can happen on the Little Red just like anywhere else. I've resorted to this technique to take some tough river Rainbows many times. The pool closest to the dam seems to have fish that demand this technique more often than not. Sample the stream in their area and you'll find out why—an abundance of midge larva in the water.

Another situation that requires a special technique on the Little Red is when the generators are running. Most fly fishers leave the river at this time for safety reasons. If you and a partner are experienced in handling a boat in high water, or better yet, hire a guide who's equipped and experienced for high water fishing, good fishing can be had. Large trout turn on when the generators are running. We have taken good fish at times, control drifting and tossing large streamers tight to the bank and behind blowdowns. Take time to investigate the newly flooded grassy shoreline. Trout will move into inches of water to feed on the rising tide. Be very cautious when floating the river with the generators running. We have found it best to fish with 1/2 to 1 full generator. Anything above that becomes too swift and pretty much rules out fly fishing.

As the fall/winter months of October, November and December come so do the schools of spawning Browns. The Browns will begin staging, suspended just under the surface in pools directly above and below the shoals where they will spawn. At times, large mature Browns will go through a series of aerial leaps and displays, all a part of the spawning ritual and not to be confused with aggressive surface feeding. Fish can be caught at this time, although don't be surprised if offerings go totally ignored. You will often witness large females being escorted to the shoals by one or more males, nipping at her side fins as they move in a circular pattern up river. At times a streamer pattern can get chased and eaten when the fish are in pre-spawn. Many times I've tossed a Zonker toward a suspended school and had a frenzy of activity as they chased the imitation. An erratic strip tease retrieve gets their attention and results. One thing I've found to be true with this is that they can become immune to the streamer after a few retrieves. The scenario goes something like this. Select a large fish or school of fish. To prevent spooking the fish, use enough leader and tippet to make a long accurate cast. Start the retrieve with an erratic stripping action. The intended fish, if not spooked will give chase, many times sharking after the intruder giving an easy solid hook up. This usually takes place early in the staging period and early in the morning before they are disturbed. After the first fish or two are caught from the school it becomes much more challenging to get a take. They begin cat and mouse chases and often swirl or short strike the offering.

Changing up speeds of the retrieve can cause a reluctant fish to overrun the streamer and commit to a strike. After they lose interest in the streamer, delicate sight casting with small offerings can at times catch fish. These large mature spawners will leave the school as the time approaches and move into the shallow currents of the shoals.

The female selects a nest site and is joined by a mature cockfish and often flanked by several lesser males and juveniles eager to mate. They become very territorial chasing away all other intruders.

At this time, flashes are often seen of the female digging out the gravel to make a nest to deposit eggs. When she begins actually laying, the cockfish presses near her side, they both stretch their jaws wide (as if yawning). The male fertilizes the eggs with a white cloud of milt. Some of the eggs are carried from the redd and are eagerly eaten by other Browns nearby. Each year we also see a few large Rainbows move up into the shoals to feed on loose roe. After the spawning period these fish separate and move to deeper water and cover to rest and regain energy. At times from fall through early spring, we find groups of holdover mature Rainbows spawning in the river. These are spectacular fish, seasoned and brightly dressed in spawning color. It's sad to see these Rainbows on the decline. With the heavy harvest on stocked Rainbows, we see fewer and fewer of these fish return to the spawn site.

Fishing during the spawning months can be fabulous in both size and numbers of fish. Many of us remember the days when only a handful were "*in the know*" on this great fishery. The numbers of anglers that gather in the shoals each fall tells the same story that happens to all boom fisheries.

But nevertheless, it can be a great time, if certain common sense rules are followed. Mind your manners, be helpful to beginners (we were all once beginners). Don't crowd or fish for someone else's fish. Learn to identify an active redd and don't wade through them. Sight cast to individual fish with a dead drift technique and small barbless egg imitations or nymphs to eliminate snagging of fish. Play, land and release fish as quickly as possible.

If you photograph your fish, have someone with a ready camera, get the pictures taken quickly and the fish revived and released as quickly as possible. (Don't keep the fish out of the water any longer than you want to be underwater.)

Handle large fish by the tail and cradle under the jaw with the other hand. Avoid fingers in the gills. Handle with wet hands. Encourage and assist beginners in a friendly manner to practice and promote these rules and we can enjoy fabulous fishing for years to come. Catch and release only improves the fishery and insures you and those who fish after you a chance at a wonderful fishing experience. If you must have one for the wall, most qualified taxidermists offer replica mounts that give you a beautiful trophy and allow the fish to remain in the river to spawn, grow and be caught again.

Big Browns can be caught all year long on the river. The spawn is a great time to fish but each year we see hordes of anglers who come in for a couple of weeks of the frenzy and hammer the fish hard and don't fish the river until the next year. Become a student of the river and know the changes in the fish's movement and patterns and your success will continue throughout the year. I have a lot more admiration for the angler who can skillfully catch a trophy fish in the non-spawn period rather than a large number during the spawn. This is a fragile wild Brown trout fishery very unique to Arkansas. It can only sustain and maintain a quality fishery through good levels of natural reproduction. Over the years the Browns have done surprisingly well. It is a fishery that we must keep a conservative eye on. If fishing during the spawn proves to cause a decline in this remarkable fishery we should be the first to act in accordance for what's best for the fish.

The Little Red can offer both novice and seasoned fly fishers a challenging experience. From stocker Rainbows and Cutthroats to worldclass stream bred Browns, the Little Red should continue to be one of the best tailwater trout rivers in America. Do your part to ensure it maintains the quality by practicing Catch and Release and encouraging others to release today and catch tomorrow.

I've been fortunate to have had the Little Red as my classroom over the past years. She has taught me plenty. It is a river I love to fish. She will challenge beyond your skill on some days, but she gives up her secrets a little at a time to those who take time to explore and observe and be a student of the river. May her waters always run cold and clean and her trout forever a challenge.

Fly Recommendations

Here is a list of patterns that we have found to consistently produce on the Little Red. As anywhere, others work from time to time, but this selection produces results.

Nymphs

Sow Bugs
Whitlock Squirrel Nymph or March Brown Nymph
Flashback Hares Ear
Soft Hackled Pheasant Tail or ginger-bodied soft hackles
Vernille San Juan Worm (red, natural or orange)

Terrestrial and Dries

Chartreuse Caddis (Leaf Hopper)
Tan Caddis
Black Ant
Cream Dry Wooly
March Brown
Cahill
Blue Winged Olive
Gray and Cream Midge

Streamers

Woolly Buggers (Black, Olive, White)
Gray Leeches
White Zonker

River Access

	River Mileage
JFK Park at the Dam	0.0
Cow Shoals	5.5
Barnett Public Access (Winkley Bridge)	9.0
Swinging Bridge Resort	9.0
Libby Shoals	13.0
Lobo Landing	15.0
Dripping Springs Landing	23.0
Pangburn Bridge	24.0
Ramsey Access	29.0

Directions to Area

Greer's Ferry Dam	#25 or #5
Cow Shoals	#210
Barnett Public Access (Swinging Bridge Resort)	#110
Pangburn Bridge	#110
Libby	#337
Lobo	#337
Dripping Springs Landing	off #110 out of Pangburn
Ramsey Access	east of #124 out of Pangburn

Heber Springs to West Memphis	135 Miles
Heber Springs to Little Rock	65 Miles
Heber Springs to Fort Smith	167 Miles

Airport—Heber Springs (4,000 ft lighted runway, tie downs available)
pick up service available

Places to Stay *on* the River

	Camping	Cabins	Telephone
Lindsey's Rainbow Resort Rt. 3 Box 89 - GFL Heber Springs, Ar 72453	X	X	(501)362-3130 (501)362-3139
Lil' Red Trout Dock Wilburn Star Rt. Heber Springs, AR 72453	X	X	(501)362-2197
River Ranch Resort Box 483 Heber Springs, AR 72453	X	X	(501)362-9003

	Camping	Cabins	Telephone
Swinging Bridge P.O. Box 183 Heber Springs, AR 72543	X	X	(501)362-3327
Lobo Landing P.O. Box 143 Heber Springs, AR 72543	X	X	(501)362-5801 (Reservations Only)

Accommodations in Heber Springs

Anderson House Inn
(Bed and Breakfast)   (501)362-5266
201 East Main St.
Heber Springs, AR 72543

Holiday Inn
3450 Highway 25B North   (501)362-1000
Heber Springs, AR 72543

NORFORK RIVER

NORFORK RIVER

NORFORK RIVER

NORFORK RIVER

Norfork River

by John Berry

The Norfork River, in my opinion, is the premier trout stream in North Central Arkansas. Less than five miles from the Norfork Dam to the confluence with the White River, this stretch of water consistently produces large numbers of quality trout for the fly fisher.

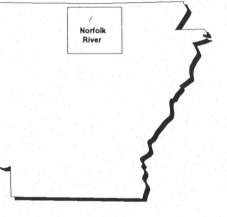

Norfolk
River

The Norfork is a tailwater river and is subject to substantial variation. Whenever you are fishing, keep a look out for rising water and always keep an escape route in mind. At low water the river is easily waded and easily accessed. There are four basic accesses: Quarry State Park (also know as the dam), McClellan's, Goats Bluff, and the Twin Rivers Tavern. In the descriptions that follow all directions are given while looking downstream.

Quarry State Park

The park is located just below the Norfork Dam on Highway #177 two miles from Salesville, Arkansas. At the confluence of Dry Run Creek and the Norfork, fish the riffle with soft hackles or nymphs. Directly across the Norfork on the left bank is a small bedrock run that always holds a few good fish. Fish a small nymph on a strike indicator. The water deepens and slows as it runs by the campground. While there is good fishing with nymphs and streamers, when the top-water action starts, this section can be spectacular especially with emergers. Downstream there are two riffles that are marginally productive with nymphs but as you near the end of the second run there is a deep hole that holds nice fish. Below the last riffle is a nice flat section that can be fished at any time with streamers on a sink tip line. This also is great midge fishing water.

McClellan's Trout Dock

This is the holiest of waters. It has without a doubt the best fishing on the Norfork...no...the best fishing in Arkansas. This is where a world record Brown trout was taken in 1989 (38 lb. 9 oz.) and the late Chuck Davidson held court and taught locals how to fly fish. Chuck is the creator of Chuck's Emerger which is deadly on these waters (see fly recipes at back of book). The upper riffle, upstream from the dock, holds good fish and is easy to wade. Use nymphs and soft hackles. This is a good place to fish at night.

The flat water from here to the point of rocks is slow. Against the right bank and it is sometimes quite deep. Long tippets and small nymphs fished with a strike indicator are the order here. At the end of the flat water there is a deep hole that holds a lot of fish. This is a great place to fish woolly buggers and to introduce novices to the quiet sport.

Just downstream on the near bank is a small rocky point. This is probably the most productive spot at this access. Wade out on the point and cast toward the opposite bank and let your fly swing with the current. Fish any fly here, nymphs, streamers, wet, or dries. Something is always happening.

Just below and to the left of the point of rocks is the "Ace-in-the-Hole" waters. This is thin water over bedrock that has deep cuts in it. These cuts provide protected lies that hold lots of spooky fish. This is emerger water and long casts using 6X to 8X tippets are required. Keep your body low and use stealth when approaching fish. This is a tough spot to fish nymphs and streamers, but wet flies fished downstream can be very effective.

Waterfall pool, just downstream from "Ace-in-the-Hole" water has a deep hole that holds huge fish. Fish this spot with a woolly bugger on a sink tip line or fish the current streams with a nymph. Below the waterfall pool two riffle currents converge and flow into a pool. Fish the inside margins of the current streams with nymphs or wets. After the currents converge, fish the main current with streamers and sink tip lines. The tail end of this pool is difficult to fish but has some good midge hatches. Below the pool is an island. The right channel has a nice riffle that is excellent for nymphs and wets. As this current tails out in the pool below the island, there is a shallow run that has numerous pockets that hold fish. Use nymphs and wets. The big pool below is the "Admiral Hole". You can wade pretty far down on the right side. This is a spectacular pool for dries, midges, emergers and streamers. This area is far from the access and you should be very careful. Plan your avenue of escape well should the water begin to rise.

Goat's Bluff (handicap access)

Goat's Bluff is located on River Ridge Road off Highway #5 just north of the bridge over the Norfork River. There is a handicap access here and the parking spaces located on the river for handicap use.

Wade upstream from the access on the near bank past the two islands to a small waterfall. Fish the current streams below the falls with woolly buggers and nymphs. From the point where the currents die out below to the second island is generally non-productive. There is good water on both sides of the second island. The left current is deeper and holds more fish. Fish nymphs, wets, and streamers here. The right channel is shallow with numerous pockets that hold fish. Use wets and emergers that are swung in the current on a floating line.

Below the second island and toward the left bank, there is a slick section of flat water that flows slowly around large boulders. This is a tough section that grudgingly offers large fish on emergers to crafty fishers. You'll need long casts and long thin tippets. There is a channel that flows through this area that is the perfect place to swing woolly buggers.

Directly in front of the access is a nice riffle that is constantly being pounded. Avoid it and fish the pool below. The right side is more productive and is excellent midge water. This is a tough place so use long casts and long leaders. Just below this pool there is a small riffle. Fish the inside margin with small nymphs. There is a ledge right below the margin that holds fish. Fish it slowly and deliberately.

For the next quarter mile there is flat water and spooky fish. During midge hatches there can be good action. Below this on the right side a riffle divides into two chutes and creates a deep bedrock run tight against the right bank. Small nymphs and woolly buggers cast toward the right bank and swung with the current are very productive. The run tails out and forms a flat over huge boulders that contain large fish. This area is best fished with emergers.

Below this and above the lower island there is a spectacular chute on the left side. Fish it with woolly buggers on a sink tip. Here again you are far from an access. Keep in mind an escape route. The cliffs on the right are steep and difficult to scramble up. The left side is on the other side from the access and would necessitate a long walk back to your car.

Twin Rivers Tavern

Just below the Norfork bridge there is a tavern that allows customers to park and fish. At low water wade up to the riffle just below the island on the right side. There is a bedrock run below that always holds fish. Fish nymphs and streamers on a floating line and a strike indicator. The river widens out with a channel on the left bank from here to the bridge. This is woolly bugger country. Beneath the new bridge is a deep hole that can be fished from the right piling. You must have a sink tip, a large streamer and lots of backing.

Dry Run Creek

Dry Run Creek is a feeder creek for the Norfork. It deserves special attention due to the special restrictions and spectacular fishing. It runs by the Federal Hatchery and through Quarry Park on Arkansas highway 177, two miles north of Salesville, Arkansas. It has been set aside for children and the handicapped. For children to fish it, they must be under 16 and be accompanied by an adult with a valid Arkansas license and trout stamp. Only single hook artificials may be used. You must not use bait and all fish must be released immediately. There is a handicap access at the hatchery parking lot.

This is a wonderful place to bring a child. There are large numbers of trophy trout and this creek is not affected by generation. The stream receives all the water from the hatchery discharge and is loaded with food. The stream is shallow and easily waded in hip boots.

Fly Recommendations

The trout on this stream frequently take to the top and dries, emergers, and soft hackles can be deadly. Nymphs and streamers are always good producers. Smaller sizes are in general more productive.

Nymphs
Sow Bugs .... #14
Red Fox Squirrel Nymphs .... #14 #16
Gold Ribbed Hares Ear .... #14 #16

Dry
Light Cahill .... #14 #16 #18
Elk Hair Caddis .... #14 #16 #18
Pale Yellow Paratilt .... #16 #18

Wet
Partridge & Orange .... #14 #16
Hare's Ear Soft Hackle .... #14 #16
Red Ass .... #16

Emergers
Chuck's Emerger .... #18
Chuck Berry's Emerger .... #18
Dan's Turkey Quill Emerger .... #18

Streamers
Woolly Buggers —brown, olive & black .... #8, #10
with flash
Wool Head Sculpins (olive) .... #6, #8

Midges
Cream, Red and Gray .... #12 - 20
Griffith's Gnat .... #24

NORTH FORK OF THE WHITE RIVER

North Fork of the White River Ozark County, Missouri

by John Simank

The North Fork of the White River is located in extreme south-central Missouri about sixty minutes north of Mountain Home, Arkansas. Kelly Ford near Dora, Missouri, where the better trout fishing begins, is approximately forty five miles north of Mountain Home, Arkansas.

This is one of the most beautiful free flowing streams in the Ozarks. The river originates in Mark Twain National Forest and is fed by a multitude of natural springs along its length and the water quality is excellent. It is an absolute jewel of a trout stream, and comes as close to a western trout stream as can be found in this part of the country. The rainbows are all wild stream bred fish and a two fish fifteen inch minimum limit insures that there are quality browns and rainbows. The fishing is far more challenging than the Arkansas tailwaters, and you are unlikely to catch as many fish as you will on the White or lower Norfork. However, the fish you do catch will be far more memorable that the usual hatchery fish. The rainbows have incredible color and fight like fish twice their size.

The river has an amazing diversity of aquatic insect life and far more hatches, both mayfly and caddis, than the Arkansas tailwaters. There are huge brown and black stonefly nymphs in the heavy riffles as well as golden stones, scuds, caddis, and mayflies.

Unfortunately, the river is one of the Ozark's most popular canoe streams. The canoe traffic in the summer time is extremely heavy on the weekends and makes it difficult to fish from April until September when the canoes thin out. You can fish very early and late in the day, and if you are a dry fly fisher there are some excellent late hatches in the summer. It is possible to avoid the heaviest canoe flotillas by moving from access to access during the day, but you will not avoid them all. Of course if you are fortunate enough to be able to fish on a weekday the canoes are not nearly as much of a problem.

The canoeable portion of the stream begins at the Missouri Highway 76 bridge in Douglas County, Missouri. For the next thirty four miles the North Fork is a warm water smallmouth stream until Rainbow Spring (sometimes called Double Spring) adds about 137 million gallons of icy spring water to the river. It is the fifth largest spring in Missouri and lowers the overall water temperature to the point that the river will support good trout populations for the next thirteen miles.

The spring itself is owned by a private club and is posted. The area just below where it empties into the river, however, is one of the best areas to fish on the river. Kelly Ford is the closest access to this area and is about one-half mile downstream from the spring. It is difficult, but possible, when the water is low, in the summer to wade up river from Kelly Ford to Rainbow Springs. The closest access up river from the spring is at Hammond Camp where Missouri highway CC crosses the river. This is about three-and-one-half miles up river from the spring.

Probably the most effective way to fish the river, when the canoe traffic allows, is to canoe the river yourself, stopping and wade fishing the riffles and runs along the way. The best stretch to float for trout fishing is from Kelly Ford to Patrick Bridge, a distance of about eight river miles. While this might seem like too long a stretch to canoe and fish, the river has good gradient (about 6.4 feet per mile) and you can easily make it and have plenty of time to fish even if you start as late as mid morning.

Ozark County, Missouri is one of the most beautiful places to fish and visit in the Ozarks. In addition to the fine trout fishing offered by the North Fork of the White, there is excellent Smallmouth fishing in Bryant Creek, a beautiful stream just west of the North Fork. There are lots of pretty places to see on both these streams as well as in other parts of the county.

Dawt Mill on the North Fork river is one of Missouri's historic mills and is still a working grist mill. It is quite beautiful and well worth a visit even if you do not stay there. It has cabins, camping, a general store, and a gift shop. They also rent canoes and provide shuttles.

Hodgson Mill on Bryant Creek is where Ewell Gibbons did his Grape Nuts commercials. It is driven by a spring that comes up out of the ground just in front of the mill. It now houses a gift shop and there are camping and canoe rentals at the mill.

Rockbridge Mill is also in Ozark County. It is a pay-to-fish trout fishing area with cabins and a restaurant. Rockbridge is very popular and it is difficult to get reservations. The restaurant is only open to guests. You can visit the mill and take a look at the trout stacked up in the stream below. It is well worth a visit. Rockbridge is located on Hwy N just north of MO 95.

Zanoni Mill Inn, just down Hwy 181 from Hodgson Mill, is another historic Missouri Mill and a very fine bed and breakfast. The Inn is the home of Dave and Mary Morrison, an extraordinarily nice couple. The rooms are huge, and one wing of the house is an enormous indoor swimming pool. Mary serves the best full breakfast there is which is included in the price of the room. Dave and Mary are related to the people who own Rockbridge and have an arrangement where they can get you in for dinner if you are staying at the Inn.

The Mill is adjacent to the house and is driven by a spring that comes out of a bluff next to it. The water then forms a lake of several acres just in front of the house. The lake has outstanding large and smallmouth bass in it as well as bluegills and crappie. There is also a creek that runs next to the house. Although it drys up in the summer, there are holes along the creek that holds Smallmouth up to one and a half pounds.

Fly Recommendations

Nymphs (mostly weighted)
Lord Gray Nymph 12-18
Beaver Nymph 12-16
Prince Nymph 10-16
Zug Bug 10-16
Midge (brown) 18-22
Montana Stone (black) 10-14
Red Fox Squirrel Nymph 12-16
Hare's Ear 10-18
Bighorn Shrimp...12-18
Tellico 10-16
Peacock & Grizzly 12-16

Dries
Light Cahill 14-16
Adams 12-18
Elk Hair Caddis 14-18
Pale Morning Dun 16-18

Streamers
Thunder Creek Series 8-12
Black Nose Dace 10-14

DIRECTIONS FROM MEMPHIS:

I-40 thru West Memphis, then I-55 north. Go 16 miles and take the Hwy 63 north (Jonesboro exit). Take US 63 for 145 miles, through Truman, Jonesboro, Hoxie (you must turn left and then right in Hoxie to stay on US 63. Don't miss the second turn), Hardy, Mammoth Springs, Thayer, MO., to US 160 near West Plains, MO. Go west on US 160, 26 miles to Hwy H (4 miles past Caulfield, MO). Turn right on Hwy H and Patrick Bridge is approximately six miles.

The junction of Hwy H and MO 181 (where you turn off to go to Kelly Ford) is about 10 miles farther.

DIRECTIONS FROM MOUNTAIN HOME:
Take Ark 201 North out of Mountain Home. (If you go through Mountain Home on US 62 turn north on Ark 5 about in the center of town. Just after you make this turn Ark 201 North veers off to the right.) Approximately 13 miles out of Mountain Home you cross the Missouri state line and the highway changes to MO Hwy J. About six miles past the state line Hwy J dead ends into US 160. Turn east on US 160 and go about 5 miles to Hwy PP just past the bridge above Norfolk Lake at Tecumseh, MO. Turn left on Hwy PP and the turnoff to Dawt Mill is about 2 miles. If you continue on Hwy PP past the Dawt Mill turnoff for about 5 miles, Hwy PP dead ends into Hwy H (you will cross over the Norfolk River on Hwy PP on the James Bridge, but this bridge is not an access). Patrick bridge is 2 miles to the right on Hwy H. If you turn left on Hwy H, the junction of Hwy H and Hwy 181 (where you turn off to go to Kelly Ford) is about 8 miles.

Points on the River...

	RIVER MILEAGE	COMENTS
Highway 76 bridge	0.0	Access better at low water bridge 0.5 miles downstream
Low water bridge at old mill at Topaz	6.6	Access point
Slab ford	11.1	Access point
Osborn Ford	12.2	Access point at low water bridge on connector road between Hwy 181 and Hwy W
Hale Ford Bridge	14.8	Access road on connector road between Hwy 181 and Hwy W.
Hebon Access	18.7	Bridge on connecting road between Hwy AA and State Hwy 14
Twin Bridges (Hwy 14 Bridge)	24.1	Fee access and camp ground
Hammond Camp access (Hwy CC bridge)	29.2	Popular put-in access for canoes. Excellent camp ground maintained by the Forest Service.
Rainbow or Double Spring	33.5	No access. Spring posted. BEGINNING OF TROUT WATER. Fifth largest spring in the state.
Kelly Ford Access	34.0	Access off of junction of Hwy 181 and Hwy H. Best spot to put in to float and trout fish.
McKee Bridge	35.0	No access. Private bridge.
The Falls	36.0	3 foot ledge that should be portaged by the inexperienced. If you are going to run it, approach from river left to a slot in the center.

Blair Bridge	39.2	Access. Low water bridge that can be very dangerous in high water. Make certain you beach the canoe and portage well before the bridge on river right. Access is approached from Hwy H just north of its intersection with Hwy PP. Excellent fishing on shoal just below bridge.
Patrick Bridge	42.1	Access on Hwy H. Usual takeout point for trout fishing float. Fishing very good both up and down stream from the access.
Dawt Mill Dam	47.0	This marks the end of the good trout fishing on the river. The dam backs up water for a quarter of a mile and there is a take out at Dawt Mill just before the dam on river left. The dam and the bridge below it are very dangerous and should be portaged. The Mill is one of the most picturesque spots in Missouri. It is a working mill and resort that rents cabins and canoes and has a camp ground.
Junction with Bryant Creek	49.1	No access. Bryant creek is a stream that is as beautiful as the North Fork. It offers 43 miles of outstanding smallmouth fishing, canoe rentals, and its own picturesque historic mill.
Corps of Engineers	49.5	Access Corps of Engineers Campground. This marks the upper reaches of Norfork Lake.

Places to Stay *on* the River

	Lodge	Camp	C Rental	Telephone
Crossroads Lodge (Off Hwy H just South of Patrick Bridge. Campground and lodge just up river of bridge) *NOTE: Archie has sold his store so you can not rent canoes or arrange lodging or camping through the store.*	X	X	X	(417)261-2642 (800)344-9472
Dawt Mill (Off Hwy PP just south of the James Bridge)	X	X	X	(417)284-3540
Riverside Canoe Rental (just below Patrick Bridge on county road 347 off of Hwy H)	X	X	X	(417)284-3043
Roy's Store (On Hwy CC just off Hwy 181)	X	X	X	(417)261-2259
Taylormade River Treks (Bed & Breakfast Tecumseh, MO)	X			(417)284-3055
Ozark County Angler's Cabin (Bed & Breakfast near Kelly Ford)	X			(417)261-2297
Pettit's Canoe Rental (At Blair Bridge)		X	X	(417)284-3887
Sunburst Ranch (Between Blair and Patrick Bridge)		X	X	(417)284-3443

Places to Stay *Close to* the River

	Lodge	Camp	C Rental	Telephone
Zanoni Mill Inn Bed and Breakfast (Eight miles South on Hwy 181 from junction of Hwy 181 and Hwy H)	X			(417)679-4050
Smith Canoe Rental (On Bryant Creek, Hwy 181 2 miles south of the junction of Hwy 181 and Hwy H)			X	(417)261-2568

SPRING RIVER

SPRING RIVER

SPRING RIVER

SPRING RIVER

Fishing the Spring River
In Arkansas

By Paul Pettit

The Spring River, located in north-central Arkansas near the town of Mammoth Spring, is one of the most scenic and one of the largest spring creeks in the country. Mammoth Spring wells up from the ground within 200 feet of the Missouri border. The spring produces some 234 million gallons of 58° water per day. This outflow enters the Warm Fork below an old, unused power dam; and, for the next eighteen miles the outflow supports trout, walleye, pickerel, smallmouth bass and bream.

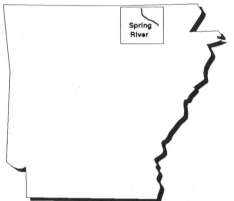

Unlike the White, Norfork and Little Red Rivers, the Spring River's depth does not fluctuate greatly because there is no power generation. However, there are other problems for the wade fisher in the form of aluminum contamination - canoes and cans. On a sunny weekend, there may be more than 500 canoes on the stretch from Dam #3 to Many Islands Camp. Quite a few of the occupants are "driving without a license" or are "under the influence". Consequently, canoes run the river backwards, sideways and upside down. While the canoes can be a hazard to the fishers, the fish do not appear to be bothered by them. I have caught and have watched others catch trout directly under passing canoes.

The river is basically a put and take fishery at this time. There are, however, a few good, holdover fish that the angler who is willing to walk a bit can fish over. The Arkansas Brown trout regulation which took effect at the start of 1990 season should ensure that everyone has a better chance of catching larger Brown trout.

Fishing the River/Access Points

The Spring River runs over a gravel and limestone bottom. Although the river's depth does not fluctuate greatly, heavy rains and consequent shifting of the gravel base change the contour of the river, its channels and the location of many of its weed beds. In many places, the gravel has been washed away leaving only limestone bottom and shelves. The limestone base tends to be extremely slippery, do not take this river for granted. Caution and a good wading staff are suggested.

Access to the Spring river is extremely limited. There are few access points and a preponderance of "No Trespassing" signs. Listed below are nine (9) public and private access points. Mileage shown is downstream from the spring head.

RIVER MILES

0.0 Mammoth Springs State Park Tourist Information Center. The Mammoth Springs State Park Tourist Information Center is located next to the spring. Going north, take the first right after you cross the U.S. Highway 63 bridge at Mammoth Springs. Although this is not really considered a public access point, you can park your car in this parking lot and walk down to Dam #1 and fish directly below the dam. Wading this section can be tricky as there are dropoffs; so, be careful.

The lake which forms behind Dam #1 is closed to fishing.

While you're there, it is worth a few minutes to tour the Center. Center personnel tell all about the history of the area and about the Spring River. On the other side of the lake is a railroad museum and a National Fish Hatchery (warm water). Both are worth visiting. Of course, take time to look at the spring.

0.25 RV Park. This is a private campground/access just downstream from (south of) the Hwy 63 bridge at Mammoth Springs.

0.3 Mammoth Spring Canoe Rental and Campground. This private campground is located just downstream from the R/V Park and consists of wooded campsites along the river. The water directly in front of the camp is nice riffle water separated by pools. The upper end of this water gets very deep; so watch your wading.

0.5 Lassiter's. This public access/primitive campground encompasses some of the best fly fishing water on the river. Lassiter's farm is located directly across the river from the Riverview Motel (see map). Access is from the road which parallels the river on the west side. Once at the river you can work your way upstream all the way to the RV Park; or, you can go downstream about a quarter of a mile until you hit deep water that is backed up from Dam #3. The remains of an old dam, Dam #2, are visible at this point. This section of river gets stocked heavily. But, because the access is so easy, it also gets fished heavily.

2.0 Cold Springs Access. This is a public boat access that also receives stocking. This section of the river is basically a moving lake - water backed up by Dam #3. The only way to fish this section is with a boat, canoe or float tube. Beware of snakes.

3.0 Dam #3 Access. This public access is a favorite among fishers. Unfortunately, it is also the major access point for the canoe liveries on the river. Dam #3 is also the location of the Arkansas State Trout Hatchery which is on a point of land directly below the dam. There are two runs below the dam: the main flow on the west side of the hatchery point and the hatchery outflow on the east side of the point. Both usually have fish. It is questionable as to which channel receives more fishing pressure.

The water from here to just below Bayou Access, some 2.5 to 3.0 miles downstream, is probably the best fly fishing water on the river, but you must be willing to walk or float it. The water contains many combinations of riffles, pools, runs and pocket water.

Note: The railroad tracks which parallel the river are posted.

6.0 Bayou Access. Located about six (6) river miles from Mammoth Spring, this hard-to-find, public access offers primitive camping sites and is popular with both the locals and the canoeing public. Directly at the access, there is some nice riffle water that flows into a deep pool and a long run. Fishing below Bayou Access really requires a boat or canoe. Working upstream from the access, there is some excellent fly fishing water.

Note: The access road is marked at its juncture with State Route 289; however, the access road takes several branches and not all of them are marked.

9.2 Spring River Oaks Camp. This private camp and canoe rental is located about 9 miles down river from Mammoth Spring. It provides canoes and shuttles. The most popular trip is from Dam #3 to the campground, about six to seven river miles. The water at Spring River Oaks is stocked with trout. There is a small fee if you just want to park and fish. Fishing is OK; but, because of the location, you will usually have a lot of competition. To get to the campground, drive 8.2 miles north of Hardy and turn left on the gravel road (just past the closed Texaco station); go about one half mile and bear to the right when the road splits. There is adequate signage to get you there.

11.0 Many Islands Camp. As its name indicates, there are many islands on this stretch of the river providing lots of holding water for trout. The fishing can be good here, but you won't be alone. It

usually isn't too quiet here either. Many Islands Camp puts the majority of the canoes in the river and donated use of some canoes to our club when we helped Mark Hudy, former state Trout Biologist, plant brown trout a few years back. Directions to the camp are the same as Spring River Oaks except you bear to the left when the road splits and go another 2 1/4 miles. About two miles below Many Islands, Myatt Creek enters the Spring River and warms the water so that very few trout are found here.

Recommended Tackle
Eight to nine foot rods for 3 - 6 weight lines. Floating lines are used most of the time except for fishing some of the deeper runs and pools when a sinking line comes in handy.

Fly Recommendations:
The following flies have proven effective for the Spring River:

Entwistle Spring River Creeper	size 10
Tellico	sizes 12- 14
Gold Ribbed Hare's Ear	sizes 12- 14
Woolly Bugger (olive or brown)	sizes 8- 12
Prince Nymph	sizes 12- 14
Lord Gray	sizes 12- 14
Sow Bug	sizes 12- 16
Golden Stonefly	sizes 8- 14

Note: Although the Spring River has prolific hatches of caddis, mayflies, midges and even stoneflies, in the past few anglers have taken fish on dry flies. However, recently anglers have had some success with dry fly fishing using Light Cahills (#14), Elk Hair Caddis (#14-16) and Trico Spinners (#18-20). Nymphs, heavily weighted, typically take most fish.

How To Get There

From Memphis (150 miles): I-55 north to U.S. Hwy 63 (Jonesboro Exit). Stay on U.S. Hwy 63 all the way to Mammoth Spring, Arkansas.

Places To Stay

	Camping	Motel	Phone
Bayou Access (no bathrooms)	X		
R/V Park in Mammoth Spring	X		
Mammoth Spring Canoe Rental	X		501-625-3645
Lassiter's (no bathrooms or hook-ups)	X		501-856-2386
Saddler Falls Canoe Rental	X		
Many Islands Canoe Rental	X	(cabins)	501-856-3451
Riverview Motel		X	501-625-3218
Spring River Oaks Canoe Rental	X		501-856-3885
Hardy Camper Park	X		501-856-2356
Beach Club (Cherokee Village)	X	(cabins)	501-856-3292

WHITE RIVER

WHITE RIVER

WHITE RIVER

WHITE RIVER

Fly Fishing the White River

Dale Fulton

The following list has been compiled to help the wading fly fisher interested primarily in fishing low water conditions. Fly fishers are most interested in fishing riffles, faster runs, areas with broken bottom structure, and current breaks, and so this list concentrates on those areas. Some points to consider when using this list:

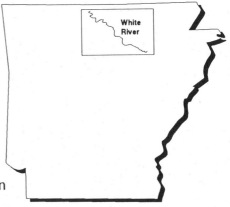

The local term "shoal" generally means a shallow riffle.

River mileages listed here are approximate; road mileage, when listed, is accurate.

Some of the accesses listed here are on private property. Although they are commonly used now, they could be closed in the future.

Because of the severe water fluctuation, the river topography changes constantly. In the future, some areas may not appear exactly as described.

Descriptions are of the river at low water. As the river rises it flattens riffles, covers islands, and changes completely in appearance.

All directions are looking downstream at the river.

Caution is advised when wading the White River. It can and does, fluctuate wildly both night and day. Do not rely on horns, warning signals, conversations, or radio reports. Watch the water, and don't hesitate to move when it starts to rise. Forego any areas that will put you in peril if the water rises. The fish in the White River are evenly distributed, and no spot is good enough to warrant any extra risk. Before fishing, call Bull Shoals Dam, (501) 431-5311, for current conditions. They will also give you generation information for the Norfork River.

White River

The White River is located near the towns of Mountain Home and Norfork in north-central Arkansas. The river begins below Bull Shoals Dam as a tailwater fishery and flows south and east to the Mississippi River in southeast Arkansas. Primary trout waters are located from the dam to the confluence with the Norfork River (approximately 44 miles). Some trout are found further down river, but bass become the predominant species as the water warms farther from the dam.

Dale Fulton, guide and owner of Blue Ribbon Flies of Mountain Home, Arkansas offers the following suggestions for fishing this excellent fishery. Following his comments, the Mid-South Fly Fishers offer some suggestions on how to get to the White River and where to stay to assist you in finding the record trout.

Bull Shoals Dam to
Norfork River Confluence

0.0   **Bull Shoals Dam**

0.2   **Upper Shoal, State Park:** Short, generally shallow bedrock shoal immediately below dam. Good fall spawning water. Access - turn from Highway 178 on to State Park road one quarter mile east of dam. Follow road to dam and park in last gravel turnoff before dam.

0.5   **Middle Shoal, State Park:** Shallow gravel shoal curving into deeper bedrock pool. Good fall spawning water. Access same as above except follow signs into State Park and park near last campsite overlooking shoal.

1.0   **Lower (Due Eddy) Shoal, State Park:** Short fast drop with good runs above and below the fast water. Fair fall spawning water. Access same as above except park in the angler's parking at the big spring overlooking the shoals.

3.0   **Cane Island:** Long shoal with medium to fast riffles and interesting bedrock ledge formations. Best water is above shoal on right and near the bottom end of shoal. Access by boat or ask permission to walk from Gaston's.

4.5   **Partee:** Short gravel shoal with pretty limestone run below. Rarely fly fished. Access by boat or ask permission to walk down from Gaston's.

5.0   **Stetson's:** Fairly slow deep gravel run to a fast gravel riffle into a deep pool. Stetson's produces many good fish for fly fishers. Access by Denton Ferry Road, also known as Rainbow Drive, (turn north from US 62 at west edge of Cotter at Wildcat Shoals Fishing Access sign), 10 miles to last dirt turnoff before Monkey Run Hill.

6.0 **Three Shoots:** Short gravel shoal with little structure into deeper ledgerock pool. Slough at top of shoal has bass and pan fish. Access by Denton Ferry Road 9.4 miles to gravel pulloff overlooking slough.

7.0 **Top of White Hole:** This used to be a nice little riffle but now is mostly shallow flat gravel. Good concentration of fish where water deepens into White Hole just below creek mouth. Access by Denton Ferry road 8.4 miles to gravel pulloff at creek.

8.0 **Bottom of White Hole:** Short gravel pour-off from White Hole. Run below fishes well but gets a lot of traffic from boat docks across river. Access by boat or scramble down bank and walk down from first pulloff at White Hole 7.4 miles down Denton Ferry road. This is a tough scramble.

9.0 **The Narrows:** Beautiful medium length section of riffles, runs, and pools, well known to many fly fishers. Access by parking in field across road from red and white barn 6.4 miles down Denton Ferry Road. Follow trail and cross dry channel to shoal water upstream. **Caution!** Do not try to fish rising water at the Narrows. You are fishing from an island.

10.0 **Tucker:** Short gravel shoal into fairly deep ledgerock pool. Fishes better than it looks. Access by Denton Ferry Road 5.5 miles, park on roadside. Scramble down bank and wade up to shoal.

12.0 **Wildcat:** Fairly long stretch of beautiful broken water, with a flat pool in the middle, well known to fly fishers. Access Denton Ferry road 4.6 miles to left spur with sign: Mallicoat. Turn left and park in cleared spot in front of can. Follow trail to shoal. Do not follow signs to fishing access. It is not near the shoal.

13.5 **Unnamed Shoal:** Short, nondescript looking, pour-off from Rainbow Hole. Produces some nice fish. Flat water just below shoal at mouth of Hightower Creek is particularly good. Access by boat.

15.0 **Hurst/Chamberlain Area:** Heavy gravel run twisting from Hurst's dock and slowing to gravel island below Chamberlain's dock. A lot of good gravel shoal and fairly deep bedrock runs here. Access by boat or ask permission at Chamberlain's 0.7 miles on Denton Ferry Road.

16.0 **Bayless Island:** Two riffles separated by a short pool. The bedrock run below the second riffle produces some very nice fish. Access by boat.

17.0 **Unnamed Shoal:** Very short gravel run just upstream from railroad bridge where side channel flows in. Better than it looks, but only in very low water. Access by parking at Cotter Springs Fishing access (turn at sign just east of bridge on US 62 in Cotter and follow signs) and walk up to shoal.

18.5 **Roundhouse:** Medium length shoal with fishable channels on both sides of island. Left channel mostly fast gravel riffles, far channel ledgerock pools into a fast riffle near end of island. Has recently become popular with fly fishers. Caution: Wading in near channel is slippery. Fishing far channel in rising water will get you stranded. Access same as above except don't take final right turn into Cotter Springs access. Stay on gravel road approximately 1 mile and park on roadside overlooking shoal.

23.0 **Redbud:** Short bedrock shoal with much deep broken bottom cover for big fish. Access—ask permission at Red bud Dock (turn at US 62 in Gassville), or walk up from Rim Shoals Dock (Turn at sign on US 62 between Gassville and Mt. Home and follow signs) on railroad tracks.

24.0 Rim/White Area: Long stretches of pretty water and the best known fly fishing area on the river. A lot of structure here was originally man-made to help shipping in the early days. Upper Rim, left of the island, is short riffles and bedrock channels. Right of the island is mostly shallow and flat with one small riffle. Large pool separates Rim from White Shoal (also called "the second island"). White Shoal is mostly shallow ledge water left of island with gravel riffles into a heavy ledgerock run into a beautiful pool on the right side. Access as above for Rim. For White turn from US 62 onto Highway 126 S. between Gassville and Mt. Home. Turn right at four way stop. Take first well maintained gravel road to right, park in space far left of white house on river bank. Wade up to shoal.

27.0 Shoestring: Long winding stretch of nice water with one fast drop. Begins just below the mouth of Crooked Creek. Access by boat.

28.5 Unnamed Shoal: Short riffle with little structure into medium depth gravel pool. Rarely fly fished and often packed with small fish due to stocking at Ranchette access just downstream. Access—turn at Ranchette access sign just east of Flippin on US 62. Turn left just before last creek bridge before access. Follow well used track across field and park overlooking shoal.

29.0 Unnamed Shoal: Short gravel riffle with some deeper water just below. As above, it is often crowded with small fish. Heavily fished by local armchair fishermen. Access—

as above except follow signs all the way to access. Shoal begins at boat ramp.

30.0 **Unnamed Shoal:** Island with gravel structure and weed beds on right. Long pool between island and Ranchette above has beautiful ledgerock structure. Slough at base of right channel has bass and pan fish. Rarely fly fished. Access by boat.

31.0 **Buffalo:** This is the longest stretch of semi-continuous shoal water on the river. It's primarily a gravel shoal, but it has a lot of interesting large rock structure and several islands. As in White Shoal, some of the structure in Buffalo was man made. The heaviest water is at the bottom of the shoal. Access—by boat or walk up the railroad tracks from Buffalo City fishing access. (Turn from US 62 as described for White Shoals but stay on paved road and follow signs to the access.)

33.0 **Buffalo Breakwater:** Gravel channels and islands formed mostly by old breakwater. Little bottom structure but not fly fished much. Buffalo River confluence is 100 yards down far right channel around biggest island, Smith Island. Access—ask permission at White Buffalo Resort just upstream from breakwater. (Same road as above but follow signs to resort as you near the river.)

34.0 **Nellie's Apron:** Hard riffle running into deeper fast ledgerock into deep pool. Produces occasional big fish but only wadable in very low water. Access by boat.

36.0 **Cartney:** Medium length stretch of gravel dropoffs and pools. Little bottom structure. Rarely fly fished. Access by boat. Road access is in the process of being closed off.

37.0 **Shipps Ferry:** Long stretch of fairly slow ledge water with good fast riffles at upper and lower end. Middle section is popular with locals because it is a stocking site. Access by following Highway 201 S from Mt. Home to good gravel road continuing straight at highway bend beyond Shady Grove Store. Cross railroad tracks and park at river, overlooking roughly the middle of the shoal. Walk tracks up or down.

39.0 **Big Creek:** Gravel island with short riffles on both sides just below the mouth of Big Creek. Rarely fly fished and has produced some big fish. Access as above to Shipps. Park and walk approximately 1 mile downstream on railroad tracks to trestle over Big Creek. Cross trestle and scramble to river.

40.0 **Unnamed Shoal:** You can miss this one easily. It is nothing but a flat water, sharp-gravel, drop off, with little current or structure, but it usually has a concentration of fish below the drop off. Access by boat.

40.5 **Matney Mountain:** Fairly long stretch of heavy water over sharp bedrock ledges. A very pretty stretch rarely fly fished. Difficult to wade unless water is very low. Access by boat.

43.5 **Unnamed Shoal:** The last shoal above the Norfork River confluence, just downstream from the Sheid Bridge. Island with shallow gravel riffles into deeper gravel pool on left, shallow ledgerock riffles on right. Usually fishes well due to concentration of fish at confluence downstream, and not fly fished too much. Access by boat.

Fly Recommendations:

Spring

Wet Patterns:	Size
Hare's Ear Nymph	12-16
Sow Bugs	12-16
Squirrel Nymph	12-16
March Brown Nymph	12-14
Shad	4-6
Caddis Pupa	14-16
Crane Fly Larva	8-10
Bighorn Shrimp	12-14
Gray Nymph	12-16
San Juan Worm	10
Glo Bug	10

Dry Patterns:	Size
Light Cahill	14-16
Sulphur Dun	16-18
Elk Hair Caddis	14-20
Midges	18-24

Summer

Wet Patterns:	Size
Hare's Ear Nymph	14-16
Prince Nymph	14-16
Various Sow Bugs	14-16
Tellico	12-14
Olive Wooly Bugger	10-12
San Juan Worm	10
Glo Bug	10

Dry Patterns:	Size
Sulphur Dun	16-18
Hoppers	8-10
Midges	18-24

Fall

Wet Patterns:	Size
Hare's Ear Nymph	14-16
Prince Nymph	14-16
Sow Bugs	14-16
Olive Wooly Bugger	10-12
BRF Shrimp	14-16
Tellico	12-14
San Juan Worm	10
Glo Bug	10
Serendipity	18-24

Dry Patterns:	Size
Hoppers	8-10
Midges	18-24

Winter

Wet Patterns:	Size
BRF Gold Matuka	4-8
Various Sculpin	4-8
Shad	4-6
Olive Wooly Bugger	10-12
Squirrel Nymph	10-12
Various Sow Bugs	14-16
Muddler Minnow	6-10
Glo Bug	10
San Juan Worm	10

Dry Patterns:	Size
Blue Wing Olive	18-20
Midges	18-24

Access to the White River

Access to the river can be found at many locations. Refer to Dale Fulton's review of fishing on the White River for specific access points.

Highways to the Mountain Home area from:

- Fort Smith/Tulsa   Rt. 40 ➜ Rt. 65 ➜ Rt. 62
- Little Rock   Rt. 67 ➜ Rt.167 ➜ Rt. 14 ➜ Rt. 5 ➜ Rt. 62

  or

  Rt. 40 ➜ Rt. 65 ➜ Rt. 62
- Memphis   Rt. 40 ➜ Rt. 55 ➜ Rt. 63 ➜ Rt. 62

  or

  Rt. 40 ➜ Rt. 55 ➜ Rt. 64 ➜ Rt. 167 ➜
  Rt. 14 ➜ Rt. 5 ➜Rt. 62
- St. Louis   Rt. 55 ➜ Rt .60 ➜ Rt. 160 ➜ Rt. 5 ➜ Rt. 62
- Springfield   Rt. 65 ➜ Rt. 62

Airport

Baxter County Airport Mountain Home, Arkansas
- Private Planes
- Lone Star Airlines Commuter Service - daily from Dallas/Ft. Worth and St. Louis

Places to Stay

Campgrounds	Camping	Showers	Phone
Bull Shoals State Park	X	X	501/431-5521
Quarry Park (Norfolk Dam)	X	X	501/425-2700
White/Buffalo Campgrounds	X	X	501/424-6892

Hotels/Motels/Lodges On the River:

Blue Ribbon Lodge   Kitchenettes/Boat Rental/Guides
960 Highway 5 South   Catered Meals
P.O. Box 1080
Mountain Home, AK 72653
501/425-0447

Gaston's White River Resort   Kitchenettes available/Boat Rental
#1 River Road   Guides/Restaurant/Pool
Lakeview, AK 72642
501/431-5202

In the Mountain Home/Norfolk area

Mountain Home Area:

Best Western Carriage Inn   501/425-6001
Holiday Inn   501/425-5101 or 1-800-HOLIDAY
Norfolk Inn   501/488-1544
Ozark Oaks Motel   501/425-9191
Super 8 Motel   501/424-5600

Norfolk Area:

Peal's Resort (Kitchenettes)   501/499-5215
Whispering Pines Motel   501/499-5331
              (Kitchenettes)
Schroder Haus   501/499-7775
       (Bed and Breakfast)

White River below Beaver Dam

by Brooks Handly

The White River...

These words are synonymous with trout fishing in Arkansas. But where on the White does the trout fishing begin?

Trout fishing begins on the tailwaters below Beaver Dam near Eureka Springs, Arkansas. Beaver Dam is the first of four dams on the river that produces trout water. This small stretch of water can be as frustrating or as rewarding as any.

I often describe this section of the White as "having no personality", but it really does, we just can't see it at normal water levels. And "normal" levels vary greatly, not only due to dam generation, but also the level of Table Rock Lake, the second in the four-lake chain. At times the lake can back up all the way to Beaver Dam.

When the lake is low, the river offers 4-5 miles of water consisting mostly of long slow-moving pools over a boulder strewn bottom. There are a few riffles and quite a few moss beds along the way, but this "structure" is not as prominent as it is in the other parts of the White River system.

Access is available from several points. The most popular are the boat ramp and rest facilities just below the dam, Parker Flats (end of county road #506 below the campground) and the highway 62 bridge. Also, on the north side of highway 62 is Houseman Access, but this is very limited, depending on Table Rock Lake's level.

Fishing "Beaver" is typical White River fly fishing using the standard patterns and any rod you're comfortable using. Woolly Buggers,

Hare's Ears, and Bead Heads on a 4 to 6 weight outfit should do the trick. At times, fishing a #14 - #18 midge pupa a couple of feet below an indicator is the ticket.

Twenty minutes to the east on highway 62 is Eureka Springs and Fayetteville is an hour to the southwest. They offer plenty of food and lodging. The Beaver Dam Store (Charlotte Downey 501/253-6154) is about a mile from the dam. Bancroft and Tabor (Bill Tenison, 501/442-2193) is in Fayetteville. Both are the places to go to pick up any information or to buy hot local patterns.

Pay-to-Fish Resorts

Rainbow Trout and Game Ranch, Inc. (Rockbridge)
Rockbridge, MO 65741
Write to: Rt. 1 Box 115
Phone: (417)679-3619
Hosts: The Amyx family

Rainbow Trout Ranch is located on Highway 95 north of Mountain Home, Arkansas between West Plains and Branson, Missouri. Follow Highway 5 through Gainesville, Missouri and travel about 16 miles north to 95. Continue about 9 miles to Rockbridge Mill and Rainbow Trout and game Ranch.

Rockbridge is a historic village settled between 1841 and 1898. This quaint and serene setting complete with old general store, the old mill, bank and church, is in the heart of the Ozark Hills nestled along a beautiful spring fed stream. It was acquired by the Amyx family in 1954. The stream is stocked with Rainbows and Golden Rainbows. The establishment allows pay by the pound, strictly no release, and no licenses. The resort will clean and freeze your daily catch. Modern cabins provide spacious, clean accommodations, for groups, individuals and families. There is a lounge and restaurant with delicious food a small tackle shop, library and game (checkers) area. Rockbridge offers all of this, as well as some of America's finest trout fishing.

FLY SUGGESTIONS:
 Woolly Buggers
 Red Fox Squirrel Nymph
 Partridge and Orange

Spring Valley Trout Ranch
Write to: Rt. 1 Box 115
Thornfield, MO 65762
Phone: (417)265-3699
Hosts: Connie and Bob Nickel

Spring Valley Trout Ranch is located in the Mark Twain National Forest between West Plains and Branson, Missouri north of Mountain Home, Arkansas, and southeast of Springfield, Missouri. Travel to Gainesville, Missouri, then north on Highway 5 to Highway Z. Continue west on Highway Z to Spring Valley.

Spring Valley offers trout fishing along one mile of a secluded spring fed stream. There is no limit and no license required. You may pay a flat daily rate to catch and release, or pay by the pound and have the staff clean and freeze your catch daily. The fishing is constantly good due to the daily stocking of Rainbow trout from the ranch's own raceways. The resort property occupies 235 acres and offers excellent meals in a dining room that is part of a modern 22 unit motel with clean and comfortable lodging. This is an excellent place to plan a family vacation, a business conference or club meeting.

FLY SUGGESTIONS:
    Woolly Buggers
    Red Fox Squirrel Nymphs
    Partridge and Orange

WARM WATER

WARM WATER

WARM WATER

WARM WATER

WARM WATER

Bass and Bream Fishing

By C. B. Nance

Some of the best bass fishing waters are within a two-hour drive from Memphis, Tennessee. There are lakes and rivers in Arkansas, Mississippi and Tennessee that will satisfy almost everyone.

For those who have not taken up bream and bass fishing with a fly rod, the following information may be helpful. For bream, the same equipment and flies that are used for trout fishing can be used. Since trout flies are generally more expensive, it is best to use so-called "bream flies". These are generally small popping bugs and wet flies. The wet flies are generally chenille with rubber legs and squirrel tail. They are readily available in almost all sporting good stores.

For bass, you will need different equipment, As everyone knows, you can spend almost anything you desire for fly fishing equipment. Generally, an inexpensive fiberglass rod with a single action or automatic reel will suffice. The principal drawback to an automatic reel is its weight. The rod should be 8 1/2' to 9' long and weight of 7-8-9. A 7 weight rod can be used for both bream fishing and bass fishing, provided the bass flies are not exceedingly large. A 7 or 8 weight rod can cast flies up to and including size 2 flies. If flies are larger than a size 2, the 9 weight is more efficient.

Leaders for both bream and bass should be approximately 7 1/2' long for surface fishing, and if sinking tip line is used for underwater fishing, a 4' leader is ample. This will get the fly down. Since most of the fishing will be in depths of approximately 8 feet at the most, the length of leader is not critical. Although any size leader can be used, it is recommended that a 6 pound leader be used for bream, as you will have occasion to pull the fly loose from logs and other obstacles in the water. A leader of 8 to 12 pounds is recommended for bass. Unlike trout, you will need to "horse" a bass from underwater obstacles and get it into clear water. In addition, you should set the hook on the bass several times after the initial setting, as their mouths are tough.

There are numerous lakes and ponds within the Memphis area that can be fished for both bream and bass - in Arkansas, Dacus Lake, Wapahocca, Horseshoe, Lake Poinsett, the lakes at Village Creek State Park, Bear Creek and Storm Creek. Dacus Lake is located just across the river from downtown Memphis and within its view. To get there, you must go over the old bridge and go under it, following the signs to the camps. There are boats for rent at Dacus. Wapahocca is located on Highway 77 just south of Turrell, Arkansas. This is a wildlife refuge, and boats are limited to 10 horse motors. At the present time, there are no boats for rent. Lake Poinsett is situated three miles southeast of Harrisburg, Arkansas. Village Creek State Park has two small lakes with trolling motors only. There are a few boats to rent. This lake is located on Crowley's Ridge just east of Forrest City, Arkansas. Needless to say, Horseshoe Lake is well known to most people in the Mid-South. It is famous for bass, crappie and bream. In the summertime, it will be crowded with party barges and skiers. Bear Creek Lake is located just outside of Marianna, Arkansas, and Storm Creek Lake is located just north of Helena, Arkansas. In addition to these lakes, there are numerous old river lakes along the White River, and the Arkansas Game & Fish Commission Lakes guide may be obtained by writing the Arkansas Game & Fish commission, I&E Division, 2 Natural Resources Drive, Little Rock, Arkansas 72205. When writing, request "The Arkansas Floater's Kit" which has maps and descriptions of seventeen mountain streams ideal for float fishing excursions.

In Tennessee, there are lakes such as Beech River Lakes located on Highways 20 & 22 out of Lexington, Tennessee; Kentucky Lake off I-40 north of Waverly, Tennessee; Lakeview which is located off Highway 61 South at the Tennessee-Mississippi State Line only two miles outside Memphis. A large part of the lake is situated in Mississippi. Also, do not leave out Pickwick Lake or Reelfoot Lake.

Needless to say, Mississippi also has a number of good fishing lakes for the fly fisher seeking a warm water challenge. In addition to Lakeview, don't overlook Sardis Lake, Tunica Cutoff, DeSoto Lake, Enid, Flower Lake and Grenada.

For Tennessee residents, don't overlook Island 40 Chute which is located in Arkansas north of Marion. Go approximately 2.5 miles north of Marion on Highway 77 and turn east over the railroad tracks. There is a large sign indicating the way, and follow the signs about four miles to Daily's Boat Dock. Boats and motors are available. The Tennessee-Arkansas line goes down the middle of this old river chute, and both Arkansas and Tennessee licenses are valid.

Fly Recommendations:

    Deer hair frogs/poppers
    Dahlberg Divers
    Eels
    Damsel Nymphs
    Zonker
    Woolly Buggers

Stream Smallmouth Fishing

by John Simank

Cold water trout fishing and fly fishing the innumerable ponds and lakes in the area accounts for almost all of the local angling experiences of fly fishers in the Mid South. Fishing for stream Smallmouth is practiced by a relatively few anglers and even fewer practice the art with fly gear. It is difficult to understand why.

The streams of the Arkansas Ozarks, Southern Missouri and Middle Tennessee offer some of the finest Smallmouth bass waters in the country. They also happen to be located in the most beautiful areas in those states. These waters get far less fishing pressure than most lakes in the Mid-South and are certainly far less crowded than trout streams in the area. It is not unusual to spend an entire summer day wading a beautiful remote Smallmouth stream and not see another soul.

It is doubtful that there is another fresh water fish that can compare to the Smallmouth. Trout are certainly a wonderful fish to catch, Largemouth bass can be explosive, and bluegill pack a lot of power in a small package. None of them, however, measure up to the feel of a Smallmouth tailwalking across a stream at the end of a six weight fly rod. They are explosive, make tremendous leaps, and have a lot of staying power.

Fly gear is very well suited for stream fishing. While some quality Smallmouth streams are narrow with a canopy of hardwoods, many have broad gravel bars with ample backcasting room for the most inexperienced caster. Even the tight streams, if you learn the right casts and position yourself correctly, can be fished with a fly rod. While the spinning rod offers advantages particularly in confined areas, the fly rod comes into its own in dead drifting nymphs and casting light flies in productive spots and holding them there. There is no comparison between the two when it comes to the fun of fighting and landing fish. The fly rod wins hands down.

GEAR, LINE, AND LEADERS

The flies typically used for stream Smallmouth are somewhat larger than those used for trout or panfish but smaller than Largemouth flies. Consequently, the best rods for stream Smallmouth are heavier trout rods or lighter bass rods. An 8 1/2 to 9 foot 6 or 7 weight rod is ideal in most situations. On an extremely windy day or when using large wind resistant hair bugs, an eight weight can be useful. Five or even four weights will work, however, if it is not windy and you are a good caster.

Whatever the weight rod, it needs to have enough backbone to throw heavily weighted Clousers or to pick up deer hair bugs off the surface. The newer third generation graphite rods with fast action tips work exceptionally well.

Most of the time floating line is best suited to streams and weight forward line is perfectly adequate. So is a bass bug taper line but it isn't that much of an improvement. Occasionally, particularly in the spring when the water is high, sink tip line in the faster sinking weights is a good choice.

Leaders need to be a little heavier than those typically used in trout fishing. With floating line, nine foot leaders with a .021 butt from 0X to 3X work well in all but very clear, slow water. The 0X is necessary for large hair bugs that are difficult to turn over and very heavily weighted large nymphs and streamers. In gin clear water late in the summer it may be necessary to go to twelve foot leaders as fine as 4X. When using sink tip, several feet of 2X or 3X tippit is all that is required. It is a real help when nymph fishing to use leaders that incorporate strike indicators.

There is no special requirement for reels. Fifty yards of backing is more than adequate and a click drag is fine.

Other items that are helpful are pretty much the same as for trout fishing: polarized glasses, hook sharpener, line nippers, landing net, a hat with a brim and forceps are all good to have along. The one difference is in wading gear. Most good Smallmouth streams have a water temperature in the low to mid seventies in the summer and are delightful to wet wade. A pair of shorts and an old pair of tennis shoes that you don't mind getting wet are all that you need. There is, however, a problem with getting gravel in your shoes and in bed rock streams with moss, it can be very slick. Several companies make a neoprene, high top, zip up boot that is very nice for warm water wading. They keep the gravel out, and, if you purchase the ones with felt soles, they help with slipping. Do not use the ones with very thin soles like the ones used for saltwater flat fishing. Most Smallmouth streams have gravel and rock to walk on and you will feel every stone through the soles.

APPROACHING THE WATER
Once you have decided on a stream you need to decide on how to approach the water. There are several choices. First, you can wade fish if the water allows and if you have permission from land owners. Some streams lend themselves to wading long stretches and you can do fine if you do not run into any obstructions or steep banks and deep pools. The only drawback is that you can only cover a limited amount of water and usually that water is close to an access point and thus more heavily fished.

If you do wade fish, it is usually best to wade upstream. The fish tend to face upstream and they are less likely to be spooked by the debris stirred up by wading. If you are going to fish downstream from the access point, try and walk the bank as far downstream as you want to fish and then fish back upstream.

Your second option is to float the stream. By floating, you can cover much more water. You can also cover water that has seen far less fishing pressure. It is also possible to fish the deeper pools that you may not be able to get to wading.

You can float from a jon boat, canoe or float tube. If it is a large stream like the White River in Arkansas (the White has an excellent population of Smallmouth as well as trout below Norfork), a jon boat with a motor is a viable option. On smaller streams a canoe makes far more sense. Most Smallmouth streams are characterized by rocky bottoms that destroy props on any type of motor.Canoes are easily maneuvered and draw little water, enabling them to glide easily over most shoals.

The best type of canoe for most Smallmouth streams is one that is made of plastic rather than aluminum. PVC plastic canoes slide easily over rocks while aluminum canoes tend to grab and hold rocks. It is also best to have a canoe with no keel and a relatively flat bottom.

One device you might also consider is a double-bladed or kayak paddle. Several companies make one that snaps apart in the middle and has T handles that snap into both ends to make two conventional paddles. This type of paddle offers several advantages. It is a more energy efficient way of paddling when one person is propelling the craft, and it is much easier to keep the canoe turned the way you want with a double-bladed paddle. A third advantage is that it is balanced such that it lays easily across your knees where you can grab it and use it quickly when you lay your rod down. You are also less likely to make a lot of noise banging it against the boat when you pick it up and put it down.

If you do not own a canoe, many times there are outfitters near the stream you wish to fish that will rent one and provide shuttle services. If there is no canoe livery in the area, another alternative is to rent one from one of the outdoor shops in the city. Most of them have foam blocks that enable you to haul the canoe on top of your car. For a shuttle you can either take two cars or pay someone near the stream to shuttle you. Leave your canoe at the put in, have them follow you to the takeout point where you leave your vehicle and then bring you back to the put in point. You can almost always find someone to do this if you offer $10 to one of the guys that always hang around the local country store.

When floating, try and limit the stretch of water to 6 miles or less in a day's float. That way you can completely cover the water without having to hurry downstream to try and beat the dark. On slow streams do a little less; on streams with more gradient you can do a little more.

The best way to fish when floating is to beach the canoe before you get to likely spots, walk the bank down and fish back up to the canoe. If you fish from the canoe, it is best for only one person to fish while the person in the stern keeps the boat at the correct angle for the person in the bow to make a back cast upstream and fish downstream ahead of the canoe. You can fish some very tight streams in this manner.

If you are solo canoeing, it is difficult to fish from the boat. You are constantly picking up and laying down your rod and paddle to try and keep the boat straight. If you want to try it, a double bladed paddle is a real asset. It also helps in controlling the canoe to position yourself kneeling just behind the mid point of the canoe rather than in the stern seat. Foam knee pads are a must for this. Kneeling in a canoe is a also good idea when floating through rapids. It keeps the boat much more stable.

Make sure you don't get on water that is too difficult for your skill level with a canoe. Streams are rated by class according to their difficulty. Class I is tame suitable for beginners while Class V is very nearly impossible to float except by experts with flotation or in covered craft. There are canoeing guides for most areas that rate the streams in that area. A list of them for Tennessee, Arkansas, and Missouri are included in the reference section.

There are a few safety tips for canoeing that will help keep you out of trouble, particularly on faster streams. If you should turn over, get upstream of the boat quickly so that you do not get pinned between the canoe and an obstruction. Overturned canoes have a tremendous amount of force when they are broadside to even a moderate amount of current. If your canoe does get pinned, don't try to dislodge it standing downstream from it.

Avoid deadfalls (tree tops laying in the water). They are dangerous. Many times they will be on the outside of bends so stick to the inside when going around blind turns. Low water bridges can also be dangerous in high water. Take out and portage well before you get to them and never try to float over one that is flooded. Some Ozark streams are choked with willow thickets. They are very hazardous in high water, and it's almost impossible to drag your canoe through them in low water. Avoid canoeing these streams.

If you want to improve your skill level, there are canoe clubs that teach basic and white water canoeing courses. The Bluff City Canoe Club in Memphis, for example, offers courses for a very nominal fee. They stress safety and do an outstanding job of teaching.

One final word of caution. Canoes eat fly rods. If its a tough stream, you may not want to take your best one. One with an unconditional guarantee would not be a bad choice. If you lay it down in the boat keep the tip below the gunnels. Watch where you sit and make sure your partner does the same.

A float tube is an alternative to a canoe. They work fine for streams that have high banks and pools too deep to wade. They will get you over the pools. They are a little cumbersome on streams and probably work best to fish short one or two mile stretches. **CAUTION:** To safely use float tubes, you **must** be in deep water. With your legs dangling down, you can easily bruise them on rocks or get snagged by trees and debris on the bottom.

FISHING THE WATER

Many of the same principles that apply to trout fishing apply to stream Smallmouth. They hold in most of the same areas. Like trout, Smallmouth like to hold in areas that are protected from the current so that they do not expend energy but are close to it so they can take advantage of the food it carries. The differences are that Smallmouth seem to have less tendency to get in very shallow water and more of a tendency to get under something: logs, rocks, ledges undercut banks, etc. Smallmouth also seem to have more aversion to direct sunlight than trout.

One of the best Smallmouth holding areas is side-pocket back eddies that form where the stream is constricted at a riffle and suddenly widens. This type area usually holds fish in the seam between the fast current and the backflow current. It is best fished downstream by casting a streamer in the fast current letting it swing into the eddy and then stripping it along the seam.

The point where riffles dump into deep pools is another excellent area for active bass. This type of water is particularly good if it contains obstructions that further slow the current. Dead drifting large nymphs or bouncing Clouser Minnows off the bottom is a good way to fish this water.

Any stream obstruction that breaks the current, particularly in deeper water, is likely to hold fish. In some streams this tends to be large rocks and in others stumps, logs, or root wads. Be sure and fish the front of these obstructions as well as behind them. Many times the better fish will hold in the small pocket of slack water that is deflected off the front of the obstruction.

Aquatic grass beds sometimes hold fish along the edge of the bed. Aquatic grass holds minnows, crawfish, tadpoles and other food forms. Smallmouth like to lay close to the edge, or in pockets and ambush what ever strays out. Many times you will see bass chasing minnows close to the grass.

Another type of structure that is often overlooked but can hold big fish is the undercut banks on the outside of bends. The current will wash out pockets in the side of the river, and tree roots will hold the soil in place above the pocket. Bass hold tight in these areas and you must get very close to or in the pockets to get strikes.

Bluff walls can also be quite good if there is current flowing along them. If the bluff has crevices, the fish like to lay up in them or under the large rocks that typically are in the water at the base of the bluff.

Springs concentrate Smallmouth in the cool water below them, particularly in the heat of summer. They are sometimes difficult to spot. Be aware of changes in the color of weed and algae growth or changes in water temperature when wet wading. Brightly colored watercress is a dead giveaway that a spring is close by.

Two comprehensive books on stream fly fishing for Smallmouth are Harry Murray's *Fly Fishing For Smallmouth Bass* and Tim Holschlag's *Stream Smallmouth Fishing*. Both books are excellent and are listed in the reference section at the end of this article. These books should be read if you are seriously interested in fly fishing for Smallmouth.

FLIES
Flies for Smallmouth fishing are usually smaller than those traditionally used for Largemouth. Many trout patterns in larger sizes work very well. The problem with fishing trout patterns is that the hook gap is not wide enough to hook Smallmouth. It is a good idea to tie patterns on shorter hooks to improve the gap to fly ratio. It is not a good idea to tie Smallmouth flies with a gap smaller than a size 6. In bass bug hooks you seldom need to get above a size 10.

Smallmouth primarily feed on three different food forms: crawfish, minnows, and large nymphs. Crawfish dominate the Smallmouth's diet in the summer. Flies that imitate crawfish do very well at this time of year. The best place to fish them is to drop them over the edge of ledges, around baseball size rocks, in aquatic grass pockets and along bluff walls. They do not tend to do well in heavy current as it is tough to get them down and they tend to wobble and look unnatural. Crawfish are not often found in areas of heavy current. They are always on the bottom so you must get the fly down to fish it correctly. The best way to fish them is to crawl them slowly along the bottom and occasionally scoot them with a quick short strip.

Dace, chub and shiner minnows are also eaten heavily by Small-mouth. They are their primary food in the early sprlng and late fall when the crawfish are not active. They do, however, feed on minnows all year and streamers are very good in the summer. Most minnows tend to be translucent and consequently streamer patterns should be tied thinly.

Clouser Minnows are an extremely effective pattern, probably because they get down so quickly. They work well in white, chartreuse, tan, and dace patterns. Shenk's White Streamers and weighted white zonkers are good chub imitations. Simple marabou jigs are often great. In waters that contain sculpin and mad toms, wool head patterns work.

There are times when the fish are chasing minnows on top when you will want to use unweighted streamers. Dace patterns (#4 and #6) with red eyes, Waterman's silver outcasts, Mickey Finns and simple chartreuse and white streamers are some patterns that work. The more brightly colored patterns are particularly effective in the spring.

Smallmouth also feed all year on large nymphs in waters that contain hellgrammites and stoneflies. Murray's hellgrammites, and marabou hellgrammites are good. Bitch Creeks, Casual Dress, Woolly Worms, and Brooks stoneflies are effective nymph patterns.

As in trout fishing, there are patterns that don't imitate anything specifically that work well. Woolly Buggers in olive, brown, black, and white are as effective for Smallmouth as they are for trout. They do better with lead eyes to get them down quickly. Patterns similar to Woolly Buggers with lead eyes, mylar chenille, rubber legs rather than hackle, and a marabou tail are excellent. Simple lead eyed rabbit strip flies with a short red crystal flash butt in white, black, brown, and chartreuse work.

Stream Smallmouth strike topwater flies readily, particularly in the summer. It is the most exciting way to fish for them. Baby doll patterns with a deer hair head, foam covered with mylar body, and long marabou tail fished like a wounded minnow are excellent. Smaller Dahlbergs with a marabou tail in black, white, or chartreuse are good. A peach colored Dahlberg with an olive head, and olive marabou tail over yellow and orange marabou with gold and copper lite brite flashing is a good pattern. The old reliable hard popper or slider does well particularly with rubber legs.

Smallmouth will also hit larger hopper patterns. A favorite one is tied with a deer hair tail, foam body, a pheasant church feather wing preened with flexament, a clipped deer hair muddler head, and madam X legs. Tan and yellow/olive are good colors in this pattern.

CHARACTERISTICS OF GOOD SMALLMOUTH STREAMS
Good Smallmouth streams have rocky rather than silt or mud bottoms. The best ones typically have baseball to volleyball sized rock which is excellent habitat for crawfish. Crawfish are the primary food source for Smallmouth and the fish tend not to do well in streams that do not support large numbers of them. Streams that contain only limestone slab rock and large boulders like you find in East Tennessee are quite beautiful, but don't contain many quality Smallmouth. There does need to be some type of large obstructions in the stream to provide cover for the fish. This can either be large rocks, logs, stumps, or root wads.

Good Smallmouth streams also have a moderate current, usually a gradient (drop) greater than four feet per mile. Streams slower than

this tend to support Largemouth and bluegills rather than Small-mouth.

Another characteristic of quality Smallmouth streams is that they have a reasonable water flow through the dry part of late summer and early fall. Many streams that look great in the spring go bone dry later in the year. Streams that almost dry up do contain fish in the holes that remain in the dry season, but they tend to be smaller, one to one and one half pound fish, and they are usually very spooky.

FINDING GOOD WATER
Unlike cold water trout streams there is an abundance of free flowing streams in the Mid South that hold Smallmouth bass. Many of them are not well known and exploring and finding them can be almost as much fun as fishing them.

Many of the State Game and Fish Agencies publish literature on the streams in their state. The literature will generally tell you what type of species are present in a particular stream and may give some indication of how well it fishes. If you are interested in a particular area, call the biologist for that area and ask him which are the better streams.

County road maps are an invaluable aid in finding streams and access points. These are usually available from the state highway departments. There are books containing all counties for Tennessee and for Arkansas that are available at most fly shops and better book stores. There are also books of topographical maps that are helpful.

Finally, there are canoeing guides for most states that contain detailed information on streams. These typically include informa-tion on the skill level required, maps detailing access points, the river mileage between access points, gradient, and water tempera-ture at various times of the year. A list of these publications is included in the reference section.

Detailed information on three of the better known Smallmouth streams follows. While these streams get a good deal of pressure, they still produce quality fish. All three are easy floats, have canoe liveries and ready access. They are good streams to get started.

CONSERVATION

Recently there have been great strides made in recognizing the critical importance of protecting our cold water trout streams. There is finally serious talk of designating portions of the tailwaters as catch and release. The folks that run the dams are becoming far more receptive to treating tailwater fisheries as something other than a nuisance. The oxygen problem is being solved and water quality is at least being recognized as a serious problem. Recent regulations on the size and number of brown and cutthroat trout are proving successful.

Our trout waters have benefited greatly from the attention of concerned fishers and conservation groups. We need the same degree of attention, if not more, for our warm water Smallmouth streams. They have been seriously depleted over the years by dams, improper waste water treatment, agricultural runoff, and siltation caused by gravel mining and farming to the edge of the riverbank. The explosive growth in chicken farming in the Ozarks has probably damaged Smallmouth streams far more than the White River.

Better regulation is needed for our Smallmouth waters. Our trout waters contain thousands of fish per mile, good Smallmouth streams only have a few hundred fish per mile and only a few of them are large fish. Stream Smallmouth have a rough life and have to fight for everything they get. Their growth rate is far slower than lake Smallmouth. It takes four years to grow a 12 inch fish in the average stream. A three or four pound fish is probably 8 or 9 years old. If a stream is over fished, it takes far longer for it to recover than our prolific trout rivers.

If you want to help, the best way is to become a member of one of the groups fighting for clean water and better regulation. The Federation of Fly Fishers has long fought to improve fishing habitat and is a very worthwhile organization. Recently there has been a club formed in Little Rock, Arkansas, which takes an active interest in preserving Ozark Smallmouth waters. The Sierra Club and The Clean Water Action Project are National groups that have accomplished a lot in cleaning up our waterways.

If nothing else, realize what a magnificent fish this is and release the ones you catch. Every time I am fortunate enough to catch a big Smallmouth, I kiss him right on the lips and let him go. It feels great.

References

State Game and Fish Agencies

Arkansas Game and Fish Commission, 2 Natural Resources Drive, Little Rock, AR 72205 (501)223-6351

Tennessee Wildlife Resources Agency, P O Box 40747, Nashville, TN 37204 (615)781-6504

Missouri Dept. of Conservation, P O Box 180, Jefferson City, MO 65102, (800)392-1111

County Road Maps

Fishing in Arkansas
(county road maps with fishable streams marked)
Arkansas Game and Fish Commission
Information and Education Division
2 Natural Resources Drive
Little Rock, AR 72205
(501)223-6351

Tennessee County Road Maps
(Available at Sporting Life or better book stores)
C J Puetz
County Maps
Puetz Place
Lyndon Station, WI

Tennessee Dept. of Transportation
Division of Mapping and Statistics
James K. Polk Building
Nashville, TN 37219
Attention Map Sales

Topoqraphical Maps

Distribution Section
U S Geological Survey
1200 S Eads St.
Arlington, VA 22202

Tennessee Valley Authority
101 Haney St
Chattanooga, TN 37041
(615)751-6277

Dept. of Conservation
Tenn. Division of Geology
Map Sales Publication Office
701 Broadway
Nashville, TN 37243
(615)532-1516

Tennessee Atlas and Gazeteer
Delorme Mapping Co.
P O Box 298
Freeport, ME 04032
(207)865-4171

Canoeinq Guides

Canoeing and Kayaking the Streams of Tennessee
Volumes I and II
Bob Schlinger and Bob Lanz
Menasha Ridge Press
P O Box 59257
Birmingham, AL 35259

Missouri Ozark Waterways
Dr. Oscar Hawksley
Missouri Dept. of Conservation
P O Box 180
Jefferson City, MO 65102

Ozark Whitewater
Tom Kennon
Menasha Ridge Press
P O Box 59257
Birmingham, AL 35259

How To Books

Stream Smallmouth Fishing
A Comprehensive Guide
Tim Holschlag
Stackpole Books
Cameron and Keller Streets
P O Box 1831
Harrisburg, PA 17105

Fly Fishing for Smallmouth Bass
Harry Murray
Nick Lyons Books
Lyons and Buford Publishers
31 West 21st Street
New York, NY 10010

SYLAMORE CREEK

Sylamore Creek —South Fork Not Just Another Pretty Face

By Roger Maler

Winding through cavernous limestone bluffs, this gravel bedded stream is one of the finest hidden treasures of the Ozarks. The Sylamore Creek feeds the White River 5 miles north of Mountain View, Arkansas. This 8.5 mile creek of riffles and deep pools is home to Rainbows of notable size and color (non-stockers). Trout are driven up by the White River high water in the winter months, returning in April due to warming waters in Sylamore. Delicate drys and nymphs are taken readily in the pocket water, fast free stone riffles and deep pools. My favorite is an olive "mini-bugger" tied on a #14 nymph hook in the classic pattern with flashabou thorax wrappings (sometimes tied with a short red tail). This is a sure killer when dead drifted and stripped for a few yards back against the current. Drys, #12 - #16 tied with any red floss work very well here, too. White wings or a parachute hackle help those with fading eyesight. Short casts quartering up stream (less than 30 feet) get the best results using 12 foot x 5X leaders minimum!

While the Spring, White and North Fork Rivers suffer from the "Aluminum Hatch" this stream is regrettably plagued by "4x4 run-off" on weekends and warm days. This probably hastens the Rainbows' retreat to the White River in April, so plan for weekday fishing and/or cold weather for the quietest times.

Just three hours from the Mississipi bridge through Marked Tree, Arkansas on Highway 63 to Highway 14, west to Mountain View, and then north 5 miles on Highway14. Where Highway 5 joins 14, follow 14 west 1/8 mile to the first left turn. Stay right on the gravel road to stream side. This is the only walk-in access reachable by 2-wheel drive vehicles. Wading upstream, fishing drys and nymphing back downstream will give you the greatest variety of fishing

pleasure. Looking deep into the heads of long pools will reveal 14 - 16" Rainbows on constant feed. Be advised, however, when you can see them, they can see you, so very quietly approach these easily spooked fish. Fishing from shore is best.

Nymphing with weighted Sow Bugs and Hare's Ears on sink tips, or lead and long 5X - 6X leaders is the order of the day. Strike indicators are optional but not recommended due to the ultra clear water and glassy surface. Fish a drift with tight line for best results.

Many inexpensive accommodations are available in the area and in Mountain View. RV campgrounds and impressive 4-star cabins are available at Sylamore Lodge (501-585-2221). Jack's Trout Dock (501-585-2211) is 1/4 mile upstream on the White River and has full service as well as reasonably priced motel rooms. Jack will portage you upstream to the intersection of Highways 87 and 14 for a 6.5 mile canoe float down to the mouth of Sylamore Creek. Plan on some walking in shallow riffles, however. Great sandwiches and outdoor seating overlooking the White are offered at Brick Shys General Store. There are also cabins available. The area's bonus is Blanchard Springs and Caverns where camping, hiking and sight seeing is awesome! Call well ahead for reservations at 501-757-2211. There are Smallmouth Bass in the lower section at the old campgrounds. In late autumn, fish with brown Woolly Buggers and Muddler Minnows.

CROOKED CREEK

CROOKED CREEK

CROOKED CREEK

CROOKED CREEK

CROOKED CREEK

Crooked Creek
by John Simank

Crooked Creek, located in North Central Arkansas, begins in Newton County near the town of Dogpatch. The Creek first flows north along scenic Ark 7 and then turns east and parallels US 62 passing through or near the towns of Harrison, Pyatt, Yellville, and Flippen. It drains into the White River below Cotter just north of the Ranchette Access.

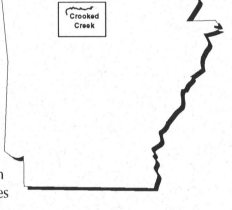

Pyatt, the uppermost point most people float, is located on US 62 about 33 miles west of Mountain Home. Pyatt is 230 miles north-west from Memphis and 137 miles north of Little Rock. The stream is about 80 miles long. The portion of the creek that is typically floated and fished from Pyatt to Yellville is about 50 miles long.

The stream is aptly named in that it meanders across north central Arkansas, constantly twisting and turning until it reaches the White River. Although it is located in a fairly populated area, it is lined with a canopy of hardwood trees that gives a feeling of seclusion. The creek, like most Ozark streams, is characterized by fast rocky riffles and runs dumping into deep pools.

Crooked Creek once enjoyed the reputation of being the premier Smallmouth stream in Arkansas and one of the best in the Nation. Unfortunately, there was little regulation to protect this valuable resource, and the fish population declined drastically. Recently, however, the state imposed a two fish, fourteen inch minimum limit on the stream, and it has responded well in both numbers and quality of fish. Although it gets a lot of pressure, it is a worthwhile stream to fish.

The best way to cover Crooked Creek is by canoe, stopping above the likely spots and wading down to them. The creek is rated a class I-II in the stretch between Pyatt and Yellville, suitable for beginners. The creek does rise rapidly after a major storm and can be very dangerous when it is at flood stage.

Clear Creek enters Crooked Creek just downstream from Pyatt and adds a considerable volume of water to Crooked Creek. Crooked Creek is generally floatable all year from this point to Yellville. Below the Yellville Highway 14 access, the creek becomes choked with willow thickets which can be dangerous when the water is high. They can also be frustrating when the water is low. Low water is usually the case on the lower stretch as a large part of the flow disappears in a sink hole below Yellville leaving the lower portion of Crooked Creek dry most of the summer and fall. This water reappears many miles away on the White River as Cotter Springs. You would be well advised to stay off this part of the river.

The best time to fish Crooked Creek is in the spring, but the fall can also be very good. Like most great Smallmouth streams, Crooked Creek has an abundance of crawfish, minnows, and hellgramites. Crawfish patterns are effective in the summer.   The fish seem to prefer minnow imitations in the spring and fall. Top water flies such as Dahlbergs, sliders and poppers are also effective in the summer.

Crooked Creek offers an excellent alternative when you find that they are running water around the clock on the White and Norfolk. The creek is very close to Cotter and there are enough access points to let you choose about any length float you want. Dale Fulton at Blue Ribbon Flies on Highway 5 South, in Mountain Home fishes Crooked Creek extensively. The shop rents canoes, provides shuttle services and experienced guides. They also stock flies that are effective on the creek. They are always happy to answer questions about the stream.

Points on River

	Mileage	
Pyatt	**0.0**	Access at US 62 bridge in Pyatt. Access is on west side of creek, and south side of bridge.

Clear Creek   2.0   Access. Turn off of US 62 0.7 miles west of the US 62 bridge in Pyatt. The turnoff is on the south side of US 62, 100 yards west of the Pyatt Baptist Church. Go 1.8 miles down the road to a cemetery. Just before the cemetery, a road to the left leads a short distance to Crooked Creek. If you continue 0.2 miles past the cemetery, you will come to a low water bridge over Clear Creek. When there is enough water, you can put in at this bridge and float 100 yards to its confluence with Crooked Creek.

Turkey Creek   10.0   This access is a little hard to find . Turn off US 62 on the south side of the highway on county road 405. The turnoff is 4.2 miles east of the US 62 bridge over Crooked Creek in Pyatt west of the US 62 Georges Creek Bridge. Proceed south on county road 405 for 0.7 miles to a small gravel road to the left. This road fords a small creek and reaches Crooked Creek about 200 yards off 405. If you miss this access, continue down 405 a total of 1.3 miles from US 62 and another small road to the left leads a short distance to Crooked Creek.

Georges Creek   13.0   Access at the US 62 Bridge over Georges

Creek, on the south side of US 62 and the east side of Georges Creek. Georges Creek is 7.3 miles west of the intersection of US 62 and Ark 14 in Yellville and 5.2 miles east of the US 62 Bridge over Crooked Creek in Pyatt. Georges Creek's confluence with Crooked Creek is about 150 yards downstream of the put in on Georges Creek. (NOTE: A new section of US 62 is currently under construction that will bypass the current bridge. When this is finished you may have to find the old highway to get to this access)

Kelly's Slab   21. 0   Turn off US 62 on county road 402 to the south, just west of the Sheriff's Department. The 402 turnoff is 3.1 miles west of the intersection of US 62 and Ark 14 in Yellville and 4.2 miles east of the US 62 Georges Creek Bridge. Continue 1.2 miles down 402 until it stops at Crooked Creek.

Yellville   24.0   Turn off US 62 onto Ark 14 South in Yellville. Access is at the Ark 14 bridge over Crooked Creek 0.2 miles south of US 62. Access is on the south side of the creek and the east side of Ark 14.

Gravel Mine
access   26.0   Turn off US 62 south on gravel road just west of the Highway Department building. Turnoff is 1.7 miles east of the intersection of US 62 and Ark 14 in Yellville and 7.1 miles west of the intersection of

US 62 and Ark 101. Go down this road 0.3 miles until you reach a gravel mining operation on Crooked Creek.

Flippin Access   **33.0**   Turn off US 62 to the south on the West side of Flippin. The turnoff is just west of the Razorback Restaurant (this restaurant is closed and may later undergo a name change). There will be a North Street and a little farther a South Street on the north side of US 62 in Flippin. The turnoff is on the south side of US 62 between these two streets. The road to the access is paved for the first 2.5 miles and then turns to gravel for another 1.5 miles before reaching a low water bridge over Crooked Creek.

Mini Storage   **35.0**   Turn south off US 62 3.2 miles west of the
Turnoff new bridge over the White River near Cotter, and 0.2 miles west of the intersection of US 62 and Ark 101. The turnoff is just west of a mini storage building. Go 2.4 miles to a one lane bridge over Crooked Creek. You have a good view of a willow thicket blocking the creek from this bridge which will give you insight as to why you have no business trying to canoe the lower part of the river.

Hwy. 101 Turn south off of US 62 3.0 miles west of
Bridge   **42.0**   the new bridge over the White River at Cotter at the sign to the Ranchette access. The bridge is about 2 miles down Hwy. 101.

Confluence with the
White River   49.0   There is no access where the creek empties into the White River. The Ranchette
access on the White is about 2 miles
down river.

Directions Mountain Home
Take US 62 west 22 miles through US 62 to Yellville.

Directions Memphis to Yellville
I-40 thru West Memphis to I-55 north. Then go 16 miles on I-55 to
the US 63 north Marked Tree, Jonesboro exit. Go 105 miles on US
6 3 to Hardy through Truman, Jonesboro, and Hoxie, (you must turn
left and then right in Hoxie, don't miss the second turn). Turn left in
Hardy on US 62 west and go 63 miles on US 62 to Yellville.

Places to Stay on the River
Red Raven Inn Bed and Breakfast
At the Ark 14 Bridge in Yellville   (501)449-5168

Places to Stay Near the River
Camp Ground Us 62B on the west side
of the White River near the old Cotter Bridge   (501)453-2299

Blue Ribbon Flies
960 Hwy. 5 South
Mountain Home, Ark   (501)430-5338

ARKANSAS

BUFFALO RIVER

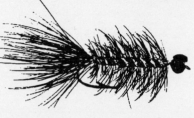

BUFFALO RIVER

ARKANSAS

Buffalo River
North Central Arkansas
by John Simank

The Buffalo River stretches 150 miles across some of Arkansas' wildest and most beautiful terrain. It was proclaimed the first National River by Congress in 1972. This saved it from becoming another in the long list of streams that have been impounded or channelized. The Buffalo remains in its natural state from its source in the Boston Mountains in southwest Newton County Arkansas until it adds to the flow of the White River at Buffalo City, Arkansas.

Buffalo River

It is truly one of the most beautiful rivers in the country. A prominent feature of Ozark streams is the bluffs they create as they cut their way through the limestone and sandstone rock of the mountains. The bluffs on the Buffalo are the highest, most dramatic and most numerous of any stream in the state. These bluffs, together with crystal clear water falls, springs, sink holes, canyons, and caves combine to make the Buffalo the premier attraction of the Arkansas Ozarks. Time spent on the Buffalo is always a treasure whether or not you catch fish.

The Buffalo is an outstanding smallmouth stream and turns out quality fish every year. Two pound fish are common, four pound fish are not unusual and five pound fish are caught occasionally. Like most smallmouth rivers it is best fished from a canoe. It does, however, offer some good wade fishing opportunities in the middle section after the hoards of recreational canoes are run off by low water in the summer and fall.

Crawfish, helgrammites, leeches, and dace, chub and shiner minnows, are abundant in the Buffalo. Flies that imitate these foods are the best bet. Woolly Buggers are also effective, particularly when the fish seem to have lock jaw on a slow day. Top water flies do very well in the warmer months.

The river begins north of Ark 16 near the town of Fallsville in the highest part of the Ozarks. For the first sixteen miles it tumbles through one of the wildest and roughest gorges in the state. Known as the Hailstone section, it is floatable only when other rivers are in flood. The water is class IV, suitable for experienced kayakers or kamikaze canoeists only.

The 30 mile upper section from Boxley to the Ark 7 access at Pruitt is canoed extensively in the spring, although there is seldom enough water to float the six mile Boxley to Ponca run. The upper section offers the best white water on the river, typically class II. It would be advisable to at least have basic canoeing skills before attempting this run.

The scenery is breathtaking, particularly the stretch between Steel Creek and Kyles Landing. This run includes 500 foot Big Bluff and Hemmed In Hollow, a box canyon with the highest waterfall between the Appalachians and the Rockies. It is common to see elk around Steel Creek and there are also occasional sightings of black bears and mountain lions on the upper Buffalo.

The river's middle section runs from Ark 7 to US 65, a distance of 43 miles. While this section is not as dramatic as the upper section, it is still a beautiful stretch of river that is a very tame class I. In the late summer and fall the part of the river between Pruitt and Woolum Ford gets very low and becomes unsuitable for most recreational canoeists. This section of river continues to hold good numbers of fish that become more concentrated in the deeper holes. It is an excellent area to wade fish when the aluminum hatch (canoes) thins out. Below Woolum Ford in an area known as round rocks, there is a sink hole that takes a significant portion of the flow underground and causes the river to run nearly dry in the late summer and fall.

The lower section of the Buffalo extends from US 65 to Buffalo City where it empties into the White River. This section is usually floatable all year and gets a considerable volume of canoe traffic in the summer from Gilbert to Rush. Below Rush there are no access points until you reach the White River at Buffalo City, a distance of 23 miles. Because it is such a long run, it requires overnight camping and consequently receives far less canoe traffic than other parts of the river. Another problem is that the take out is on the White River several hundred yards upstream from the mouth of the Buffalo. When they are running eight generators on the White, it can be quite a challenge reaching the Buffalo City access.

The Rush to Buffalo City section is great water to fish if you have two nights you can spend on the river. It contains some of the highest and most spectacular bluffs on the Buffalo. The river is bounded by the Lower Buffalo and Leatherwood Wilderness Areas which comprise some of Arkansas' wildest country. In the fall, when the trees are in full color, every bend in the river offers a new post card vista. It holds good numbers of respectable largemouth in the slower pools and pockets as well as excellent populations of quality smallmouth in the back eddies of the riffles, around stream obstructions and at the undercut banks. The fishing can be fantastic if you catch them when they are on a feeding frenzy before they become dormant in the winter.

The river is controlled by the National Park Service and all roads to access points are well marked. You should have little trouble finding them with the enclosed map. The park service allows primitive camping on gravel bars in the river. If you are looking for more refined accommodations, there are a number of lodging and improved camp grounds at major access points.

If you plan to camp on the river, check the weather. One deluge resulted in the river rising more than twenty feet in a day from the mountain runoff. It can come up very quietly at night. Make sure your boat is well out of the water or you may end up having to hike out.

If you are looking for a good guide, Duane Hada at the Woodsman in Fort Smith, Arkansas would be an excellent choice. Duane grew up in Jasper, Arkansas just south of the Pruitt access and has fished the River all his life. Duane and his wife Marlene operated a fly shop on the Little Red River for several years and he is arguably the best fly fishing guide for trout on that river. His heart, however, is in fly fishing for Arkansas stream smallmouth, and he probably knows every good smallmouth stream in the state. Although he is located in Ft. Smith, he frequently guides in the middle part of the state.

Marlene also guides on occasion. She is the answer for you ladies who don't like us men telling you what to do. If you are a male chauvinist, stay away from her. She will humble you with a fly rod.

Directions Memphis to Buffalo Point Near Ark Hwy 14 (lower Buffalo)

I-40 thru West Memphis to I-55 North. Go 16 miles down I-55 to the US 63 north Marked Tree/Jonesboro exit. Go 18 miles down US 63 to the Payneway Ark Hwy 14 exit. Follow Ark Hwy 14 west for 150 miles through Harrisburg, Newport, Batesville, Mountain View, to the Ark Hwy 14 bridge over the Buffalo which is about six miles north of Harriett, Arkansas. About one mile north of the bridge, take a right on Ark Hwy 268 and follow the signs about 3 miles to the Buffalo Point camp ground and access.

Directions Memphis to Pruitt, Ark Hwy 7 Access (Upper & Middle Sections

Take I-40 through Little Rock to the Russellville, Ark Hwy 7 north exit. Go North on Hwy 7 for 65 miles to bridge over Buffalo. The bridge is about 6 miles north of Jasper, Arkansas.

POINTS ON RIVER (UPPER SECTION)	MILEAGE	
Boxley Access	0.0	Near the Junction of Ark Hwy 21 & Ark Hwy 23
Lost Valley Recreation Area	5.0	Off Ark Hwy 43 about 3 miles west of Ponca.
Ponca Access	6.0	On Ark Hwy 43 one mile south of Ark Hwy 74 .
Steel Creek Access	8.5	Road leading off Ark Hwy 74, 3 miles east of Ponca.
Kyles Landing	16.1	5 miles west of Jasper on Ark Hwy 74 then 3 miles down a very rough road.
Erbie	22.0	6.5 miles west on road leading off Ark Hwy 7 about 4 miles north of Jasper.
Ozark	20. 6	Road leading off Ark Hwy 7 about one mile south of the river.
Pruitt Landing	29 . 6	5 miles north of Jasper on Ark Hwy 7, hen 2 miles down a gravel road.
(MIDDLE SECTION)		
Hasty	37 .1	Access at low water bridge 2 miles down a road that leads to Hasty, Arkansas off Ark Hwy 74 about 5 miles east of Jasper.
Carver	40.9	10 miles east of Jasper on Ark 74 then 2.5 miles North on Hwy 123 .
Mt. Hersey	47.9	Access 6.5 miles down a gravel road that leads off Ark Hwy 123 about 2 miles north of Hasty.
Woolum	56.4	Access 8.5 miles down a gravel road off US 65 at Pindall, Arkansas.

Tyler Bend	71. 6	Access on road leading off US 65 about one mile south of the US 65 Bridge over the Buffalo.
Grinders Ferry US 65 Bridge	72.9	Access at US 65 bridge about 9 miles north of Marshall, Arkansas.
(LOWER SECTION)		
Gilbert	77.1	Road to access leads off US 65 about 2 miles north of the US 65 bridge over the river.
Maumee - North	89 .1	Road to access leads off Ark Hwy 14 at the town of Caney, Arkansas about 5 miles north of the Ark Hwy 14 Bridge.
Maumee - South	89.1	The road to Maumee, South is 6 miles from Marshall on Ark Hwy 27 at Morning Star, Arkansas then 6 miles down a road to the river.
Dillard ' s Ferry Hwy 14 Bridge	98. 6	Access is at the Ark Hwy 14 Ark Bridge about 16 miles south of Yellville. Access is on the west side of the bridge, south side of the river.
Buffalo Point	100.1	Access is 3 miles down Ark 268 which leads off Ark Hwy 14 about 2 miles north of the bridge over the Buffalo.
Rush Landing	107.6	Access is at the old abandoned mining town of Rush 8 miles down county road 26 which leads off Ark Hwy 14 about 14 miles south of Yellville.
Buffalo City	130.6	The Buffalo City access is actually on the White River about 1/4 mile upriver from the mouth of the Buffalo. It is located on Ark Hwy 126 which intersects US 62 between Gasville and Mountain Home.

TENNESSEE

BUFFALO RIVER

BUFFALO RIVER

TENNESSEE

Buffalo River
Middle Tennessee
by John Simank

The Tennessee Buffalo is located east of the Tennessee River in Middle Tennessee. It is one of the few rivers of its size in the state that has not been dammed, flowing 117 miles in its natural state through a sparsely populated area. Flatwoods, which is located near the midpoint of the river, is approximately 162 miles from Memphis.

While the Tennessee Buffalo is not as dramatic as the Arkansas Buffalo, it is a very pretty river. It has a lush green beauty all its own and is characterized by long pools interspersed with quick, easy riffles. There are many pleasing bluffs along the river. While there is some development, it is not so much that it detracts from the feeling that you are getting away from it all.

The river begins near the town of Henryville, Lawrence County, just east of the Natchez Trace. From there it flows west to the small town of Flatwoods in extreme southern Perry County. The river then turns north flowing through the towns of Linden and Lobelville before it empties into the Duck River just before that river joins the Tennessee River near New Johnsonville.

The Buffalo has a reputation for being one of the finest smallmouth streams in the state. The upper section, the fifty four miles from Henryville to Flatwoods, has the best smallmouth population. The river has an average gradient of almost five feet per mile in this section and many springs, shoals, and bluffs which is ideal habitat for smallmouth and Redeye (Rockbass). Beyond Flatwoods, the river swings north and the gradient drops to less than three feet per mile. The lower section of the river becomes larger and more sluggish. The habitat below Flatwoods is more conducive to large-mouth, bluegill and catfish, and there is some good fishing for those species on the lower part of the river.

As is true of most streams, the best way to fish the Buffalo is to canoe it. It is all class I (suitable for beginners). The river has numerous access points that offer just about any length of float you want. Six to eight miles is about right if you have all day and want to thoroughly cover the water. The first fifteen miles of the river, from Henryville to the Metal Ford access on the Natchez Trace, is generally floatable only in the spring or after a very heavy rain.

Some of the access points are a little difficult to find as many of the roads are not well marked. However, with the enclosed map, a little patience, and a willingness to ask directions, you should be able to find all of them. Also, as is the case with most pretty streams, canoe traffic can be very heavy in the summer, particularly on weekends. Fishing early or late is your best bet in the summer. Floating during the week or fishing after Labor Day is best of all.

The best places to rent canoes for the upper part of the river are at the Bell bridge, where Hwy 13 crosses the river north of Waynesboro, or in the town of Flatwoods. Topsy Bridge to Bell bridge is a good stretch of water to fish. Bell Bridge to Slink Shoals is also good, but a little long. If you want to float and fish the extreme upper sections, you can make arrangements with the canoe liveries. It is a very long shuttle for them, however, and they will probably want to charge extra.

The food chain is not appreciably different from the Arkansas streams. The smallmouth feed heavily on crawfish in the summer Dace and chub minnows are good all year but are favored in the early spring and fall. The fish also feed to a lesser extent on hellgrammites and other large nymphs. Crawfish imitations, Clouser Minnows, Shenk's White Streamers, and Murray's Hellgrammites are all good. During the late spring and summer, when the fish become active near the surface, Dahlbergs, baby dolls, poppers and occasionally grasshopper imitations are effective. Olive, brown or black lead eyed woolly buggers are also a good choice, particularly when the fish are not aggressive.

Directions Memphis to Flatwoods

Take I 40 east 91 miles to TN 412 exit (about six miles past Jackson) Take TN 412 east 55 miles through Lexington and Parsons to Linden. Take TN 13 south out of Linden approximately 13 miles to Flatwoods.

Points on River	Mileage	Comments
Henryville Bridge	0.0	Access just east of Henryville on county road 6230.
Barnesville Bridge	5.0	Access 2 miles west of Barnesville. The access is off the road between Napier and Barnesville. Turn on an old road leading to a washed out, low water bridge.
Metal Ford on the Natchez Trace	15.0	Access. Popular picnic area on the Natchez Trace. The river goes over a series of ledges here, and it is a very pretty spot. You have to carry your canoe a short distance from the parking lot to reach the river.
Grinders Creek	19.0	Access at low water bridge on county road 6196 just off Napier Lake road.
Little Buffalo River	22.0	No Access. Little Buffalo river enters from the south on river left. This creek is periodically stocked with trout by Tennessee Wildlife Resources and occasionally they find their way to the Buffalo.

Texas Bottom Bridge	23.5	Access is just off Hwy 99 at a low water bridge on Schler road about 4 miles. Just east of the community of North Riverside.
North Riverside	26.5	Access is at a low water bridge just downstream from a new concrete bridge in the community of North Riverside.
Fortyeight Creek	36.0	Fortyeight creek enters from the south on river left. There is an access on an unimproved dirt road just past the mouth of the creek. Fortyeight Creek is a pretty good smallmouth stream.
Topsy Bridge	36.5	Access beside concrete bridge on the North side of the river in the community of Topsy.
Bartley Bridge	42.0	Access at Big Possum Creek. Reached by taking the first right off of Hwy 13 north of the Bell Bridge. Access is on the north side of the river, east side of the bridge.
Green River	43.5	Green River enters from the south on river left. The river is not much more than a small creek, but it fishes well.

Bell Bridge	44.0	Access where TN Hwy 13 crosses the river 13 miles north of Waynesboro and 6 miles upriver from Flatwoods. The access is on the south side of the river on the east side of the bridge. There are two canoe liveries here on the North side of the bridge. One with camping facilities and an RV park.
Slink Shoal	54.0	Access about 2 miles east of Flatwoods. Turn on paved road in the center of town off of Hwy 13. Buffalo River Canoe Rental Co. is located on this road and maintains a camp ground at Slink Shoals.

Places to Stay on the River

	Camping	Canoes	Phone
Buffalo Shoals Located on Hwy 13 on north side of river, at east side of Bell Bridge.	X	X	
Crazy Horse Canoe & RV Park Located on TN Hwy 13 on north side of river, at west side of Bell Bridge.	X	X	(615) 722-5213
Buffalo River Canoe Rental Co. Located in Flatwoods off TN Hwy 13 on road to Slink Shoals	X	X	(615) 589-2755
Flatwoods Canoe Base Located on TN Hwy 13 in the town of Flatwoods	X	X	(615) 589-5661

GUIDES

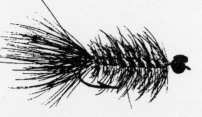

RESOURCES

RESOURCES

GUIDES

Resources for
Fishing Guides and Services

There are many resources available to assist you learn how to fly fish or to improve your skills. The following is a partial listing of the many guides and services available. Check your local Yellow Pages for other listings of fly shops/guides. The Mid-South Fly Fishers recognize that this is a changing market and that this list is far from complete.

Blue Ribbon Flies
Dale Fulton (owner)

960 Highway 5 South
P.O. Box 1080
Mountain Home, Arkansas 72653
501/425-0447

John B. Gulley
Orvis Endorsed Guide in
Arkansas

Riverview Road
Box 3012
Norfork, Arkansas 72658
501/499-7517

Gaston's White River Resort

#1 River Road
Lakeview, Arkansas 72642
501/431-5202

Berry Brothers Guide Service

1502 Harbert Avenue
Memphis, Tennessee 38104
901/726-5025

The Woodsman
Duane Hada

#153 Central Mall
Fort Smith, Arkansas 72903
501/452-3559

The Sporting Life

Chicasaw Oaks Plaza
3092 Poplar Avenue
Memphis, Tennessee 38111
901/324-2383

Ozark Angler

400 North Bowman
Little Rock, Arkansas 72211
501/225-6504

PJ's Resort

(Bed & Breakfast) 501/499-7500

FLIES • RECIPES

Effective fly fishing requires many things, not the least of which is the correct fly. The following 24 flies have been identified by members of the Mid-South Fly Fishers as key flies to have in your fly box when fishing our home waters. Drawn by club member and fly fisher **Phyllis Bailey**, recipes are included for those of you who like to tie your own. Start with these and add your own favorite flies to make every fishing trip successful and fun.

FLIES • RECIPES

RECIPES

FLIES • RECIPES

Beadhead Caddis Pupa (weighted wet fly)

Hook: nymph or standard wet fly; sizes 14-16
Head: Bead threaded over hook
Weight: light weighting wire
Thread: Cream or light brown
Rib: Crystalflash
Body: Cream, light brown, dark brown, or light yellow dubbing

Blue Winged Olive Parachute (dry fly)

Hook: Dry fly; sizes 14-24
Thread: Olive 6/0 or 8/0
Tail: Blue Dun hackle fibers
Body: Olive dubbing
Wing: Calf body hair (tied wing post fashion)
Hackle: Blue Dun (wrapped around wing post)

Chuck's Emerger (wet midge, fished in the film)

Hook: Dry fly, sizes 18-24
Thread: Orange
Tail: Wood duck breast or flank
Body: Golden yellow
Rib: Brown thread
Hackle: Ginger

Clouser Minnow (wet fly)

Hook: Scud size 14; or 1X wet fly - sizes 10-14
Thread: White
Eyes: Gold bead chain; hold chain over hook, tie on; then clip chain leaving bead on either side
Tail/Body/Beard: 8 strands of pearlescent crystalflash; tie in tail (length of hook); bring thread to front; then with same eight strands of crystalflash, taper the body up to bead eyes and once over bead to behind eye; secure to hook; turn hook upside and turn down the crystalflash to form a beard which extends to the point of the hook; tie off and clip.

Dahlberg Diver (bass and panfish fly)

Hook:	Stinger hook for bassbugs and streamers; sizes 1/0-10
Thread:	Black
Hook Guard:	30-lb monofilament
Underwing:	Peacock herl and flashabou strands
Overwing:	Olive marabou
Sidewing:	Olive-dyed badger hackles
Collar:	Black-dyed deer body hair
Head:	Rear half black deer hair; front half green deer hair

Dan's Turkey Quill Emerger (midge)

Hook:	Dry fly; sizes 18-20
Thread:	Brown, 6/0
Body:	Three (3) strands of dark brown turkey tail fibers tied in by tip
Rib:	6X monofilament
Wing:	Cream poly dubbing formed into noodle and cut short —about 1/3 body
Head:	Bronze peacock herl

Dave's Hopper (dry fly)

Hook:	2x long; 4-12
Thread:	Brown
Tail:	Deer or elk, dyed red, tied short
Rib:	Yellow thread
Body:	Yellow Antron yarn (or closed-cell foam), palmered with brown saddle hackle
Underwing:	Deer, dyed pale yellow, tied downwing style over body
Overwing:	Turkey quill tied downwing style, flat over underwing and body (lacquered and trimmed to shape)
Legs:	Grizzly hackly dyed yellow, ttrimmed and knotted
Collar:	Deer, well-barred natural dun-brown
Head:	Deer or caribou, trimmed to shape

Elk Hair Caddis (dry fly)

Hook:	Dry fly; sizes 16-22
Thread:	Brown
Body:	Brown dubbling
Hackle:	Brown, tip tied in at bend of hook and hackle palmered to head
Wing:	Elk hair stacked and tied down at head, butts clipped short

Entwistle (Spring River) Creeper (weighted)

Hook:	3-4x nymph hook; sizes 10-12; weighted with 12-15 turns of #2 buss fuse wire
Thread:	Brown
Tail:	Red fox squirrel back
Body:	Brown mink
Rib:	2-3 strands orange embroidery floss, twisted (alternative: oval gold)
Wing:	Wood duck flank (alternatives: merganser flank or dyed mallard
Hackle:	Brown or ginger folded hackle

Gold Ribbed Hare's Ear (weighted or unweighted)

Hook:	1x heavy for weighted fly, standard dry fly hook for unweighted fly; sizes 8-18
Thread:	Brown
Tail:	Small bunch of hare's ear mask
Abdomen:	Dubbed hare's ear mask
Rib:	Oval goald or, on small sizes, gold wire
Thorax:	Hare's ear mask, dubbing loop technique
Wing Case:	(optional) turkey
Hackle:	(optional) brown hen neck or saddle

Gray Nymph (weighted)

Hook:	1x heavy; sizes 10-18
Thread:	Gray
Tail:	Gray hackle fibers
Body:	Gray fur (muskrat)
Rib:	(optional) oval silver/silver wire
Hackle:	Gray hen neck or saddle

Light Cahill (dry fly)

Hook:	Dry fly; sizes 14-18
Thread:	Cream
Tail:	Ginger hackle fibers
Body:	Cahill cream
Wing:	Wood Duck flank
Hackle:	Ginger

Muddler Minnow (wet fly, weighted)

Hook:	Wet fly, sizes 1/0 - 12
Thread:	Brown
Tail:	Mottled turkey quill
Body:	Flat gold tinsel
Underwing:	Gray squirrel tail
Overwing:	Deer hair, tied in as collar
Head:	Deer hair, spun and clipped

Parachute Adams (dry fly)

Hook:	Dry fly, sizes 12-18
Thread:	Gray
Wing:	White calf, parachute style
Tail:	Grizzly and brown hackle fibers
Body:	Gray dubbing - muskrat, Antron, or poly
Hackle:	Grizzly and brown, parachute style

Partridge and Orange (soft-hackle wet fly)
(also Partridge and Green and Partridge and Yellow)

Hook:	Wet fly; sizes 10-16
Thread:	Orange
Body:	Orange silk floss
Thorax:	Mixed fur from hare's face (optional)
Hackle:	Brown partridge

Peacock Snail (wet fly, weighted)

Hook:	Standard wet fly, sizes 10-14
Thread:	6/0 olive, brown, or black
Body:	Peacock herl; robust cigar shape; weighted with lead wire
Rib:	32 guage copper wirre twisted with herl
Hackle:	Brown dry fly hackle applied for-and-aft style: three truns at rear of body and three or four turns at front of body

Pheasant Tail Nymph (weighted or unweighted)

Hook:	1x heavy for weighted fly; standard dry fly for unweighted fly; sizes 10-18
Thread:	Brown
Tail:	Cock pheasant tail fibers
Abdomen:	Pheasant tail fibers
Rib:	Copper wire
Thorax:	Cock pheasant tail fibers
Wing Case:	Peacock

Prince Nymph (weighted)

Hook:	1x heavy; sizes 8-18
Thread:	Brown
Tail:	Brown goose biot (2)
Body:	Peacock
Rib:	Oval silver
Wing:	White goose biot (2)
Hackle:	Brown hen neck or saddle

Red Ass (soft hackle wet fly)

Hook:	Scud; #14-20
Thread:	Red
Body:	Peacock herl
Hackle:	Partridge

Red Fox Squirrel Nymph (weighted)

Hook:	1x heavy; sizes 10-18
Thread:	Brown
Tail:	Red Squirrel back fibers
Abdomen:	Red Squirrel belly fur (may be mixed with clear antron for a binder) or Fox Squirrel belly colored camel
Rib:	Oval gold or gold wire
Thorax:	Dubbed Red Squirrel back fur
Hackle:	(optional) Brown hen neck or saddle

Sow Bug (weighted)

Hook: 1x heavy standard; sizes 10-18; flatten top and bottom of weight material with pliers
Thread: Gray
Tail: 2 gray goose biots
Body: Gray antron
Shellback: (optional) clear plastic baggy
Rib: Fine silber or gold wire or 5x tippet material

Tellico (weighted or unweighted)

Hook: 1x heavy wire, sizes 10-18
Tail: Grizzly hackle fibers or Guinea hackle fibers
Body: Yellow floss
Rib: Peacock herl
Shellback: Pheasant tail (alternatives: turkey, black plastic tape, black garbage bag strip, goose quill, raffia or swiss straw)
Hackle: Brown

Woolhead Sculpin (weighted or unweighted streamer)

Hook: 1-3x nypmph; sizes 2-8
Thread: Brown monocord
Body: Tan wool yarn
Rib: Gold wire
Wing: Strip of rabbit fur, tan collar
Head: Clumps of tan wool, bound to the hook shank and trimmed

Woolly Bugger

Hook: Mustad 79580 or Dai-Riki sizes 6-12
Weight: Lead eyes and or .30 lead wire
Thread: To match body color or red
Thorax: Olive, black, brown or tan.
Tail: Marabou
Hackle: To match tail plamered style
Body: Chenille or dubbing color of choice
Accents: Sparkle added to the tail and body with flashabou or crystal flash
Variations: black, olive, gray, peacock, rust, grizzly,

Notes

For Additional Copies of *Home Waters*

For additional copies of this publication or other Impressions Ink publications, please return to the location where this book was purchased. If it was purchased while traveling or was given as a gift, we will be happy to suggest a store in your area that carries our publications. Call 901-388-5382, 8:00 a.m. to 5:00 p.m., CST, Monday-Friday.

To Order Direct:

	Specify Qty:
Home Waters..$14.95 *per copy plus $4.00 shipping & handling*	_____
Mid-South Fly Fishers Club Hat..........................$13.00	_____
Mid-South Fly Fishers Club Pin...........................$ 5.00	_____
Mid-South Fly Fishers Club Patch.......................$ 5.00	_____

Please make checks payable to Mid-South Fly Fishers

Mail To:

Impressions Ink • 5147 Patrick Henry Dr. • Memphis, TN 38134

Ship To:

Name: _____

Mailing Address: _____

City: _____ State: _____ Zip:_____

Daytime Phone No. _____ Evening Phone No. _____

To Charge: ☐ MasterCard   ☐ VISA

Card Number: _____ Exp. Date: _____

Signature of Card Holder: _____

How did you receive your copy of *Home Waters?*

☐ Purchased in Retail Store

Store Name _____ City_____State_____

☐ Received as a Gift   Other *(please specify)* _____

All of the members of The Mid-South Fly Fishers want to thank you for your interest in *Home Waters*.

Proceeds earmarked for conservation and education efforts to improve area fisheries.